John Steinbeck's Fiction Revisited

Twayne's United States Authors Series

Frank Day, Editor

Clemson University

TUSAS 638

JOHN STEINBECK IN CALIFORNIA, 1938.

John Steinbeck's Fiction Revisited

Warren French

University College of Swansea, Wales

Twayne Publishers • New York
Maxwell Macmillan Canada • Toronto
Maxwell Macmillan International • New York Oxford Singapore Sydney

John Steinbeck's Fiction Revisited
Warren French

Twayne Publishers   Maxwell Macmillan Canada, Inc.
Macmillan Publishing Company   1200 Eglinton Avenue East
866 Third Avenue   Suite 200
New York, New York 10022   Don Mills, Ontario M3C 3N1

Library of Congress Cataloging-in-Publication Data
French, Warren G., 1922–
John Steinbeck's fiction revisited/Warren French.
p. cm.—(Twayne's United States authors series; TUSAS 638)
Includes bibliographical references and index.
ISBN 0-8057-4017-1 (alk. paper)
1. Steinbeck, John, 1902–1968—Criticism and interpretation. I. Title.
II. Series.
PS3537.T3234Z65 1994
813'. 52—dc20   93-47472
          CIP

The paper used in this publication meets the minimum requirements of American
National Standard for Information Sciences—Permanence of Paper for Printed Library
Materials, ANSI Z39.48-1984.⊚™

10 9 8 7 6 5 4 3 2 1

Printed in the United States of America.

Once again
for Tetsumaro Hayashi and Preston Beyer,
for their long and devoted service
to the reading and study of John Steinbeck,
especially through
the International John Steinbeck Society
and the Steinbeck Quarterly

Contents

Preface

This is the third book about John Steinbeck that I have contributed to this series. The first was specially commissioned to help launch the series in 1961, before Steinbeck's last novel was published, before he won the Nobel Prize, and at a time when his critical reputation was at one of its lowest points. In the preface I explained an intention to focus on "three general tendencies that have done most to shape his fiction," tendencies that had already received scattered attention—his obsession with allegory, his preoccupation with nonteleological thinking, and his affinities with the nineteenth-century American transcendentalists Emerson and Thoreau, though he denied any direct influence.

After his death in 1968, a need to revise and expand this work to make some kind of definitive statement about his achievement led to a new book that did not just update the former one but reviewed his whole canon from a different viewpoint in 1974. Although at that time of a review of national priorities after the American involvement in Vietnam some commentators, including Steinbeck's son John, spoke of him as "the conscience of America," I argued that during a period when there was great concern about consciousness-raising in personal and political affairs he might more accurately be perceived as producing "dramas of consciousness," employing a phrase originated by Henry James in his preface to the New York edition of his early novel *Roderick Hudson.*

Shortly after this book was published, however, when I was asked to present a retrospective judgment on Steinbeck at a conference on his "Prophetic Vision of America," held in conjunction with the celebration of the national bicentennial in 1976, I decided that the most productive approach would be to examine his work in relation to the large body of influential work regarded as modernist that had been published during the first three-quarters of this century. I outlined a concept of his relationship to other writers,[1] but as time passed and as the end of the century and the centenary of Steinbeck's birth in 1902 approached, I grew steadily more convinced that a thoroughgoing reexamination of his writings should be made in order to speculate on what his permanent place might be in twentieth-century American literature, particularly in view of his remaining one of the most widely read American authors of this century despite the reservations of many critics, especially those influential ones associated with what has been called the Eastern Ivy League Establishment.

Just as I was beginning this project, one of the most ambitious of these critics, Harold Bloom, provided a narrow focus for it by including in his Modern Critical Views series—collections of essays about all the writers he considers most important to this century—a volume devoted to Steinbeck, introducing it with the sweeping statement that Steinbeck's "best novels came early in his career: *In Dubious Battle* (1936), *Of Mice and Men* (1937), *The Grapes of Wrath* (1939). Nothing after that, including *East of Eden* (1952), bears rereading."[2] Concluding that "Steinbeck is not one of the inescapable American novelists of our century" (judged alongside Willa Cather, Theodore Dreiser, William Faulkner, Ernest Hemingway, F. Scott Fitzgerald, Nathanael West, Ralph Ellison, and Thomas Pynchon), Bloom adds, "yet there are no canonical standards worthy of human respect that could exclude *The Grapes of Wrath* from a serious reader's esteem" (5).

I am not entirely in agreement with Bloom, as will be apparent from the following critique, but in view of the scope of Bloom's work and reputation, his judgment is likely to be so widely circulated and influential that it must be kept in mind by future Steinbeck critics. Particularly the test of "rereading" that he imposes as the crucial criterion must always be kept in mind, for no matter how well intended fiction may be, it is unlikely to be taken from the shelf often if it fails to come to life for successive generations.

To concentrate on the problems that this test involves, this book will also differ from its predecessors in being devoted exclusively to Steinbeck's fiction. Because of the volume of his work, his nonfiction has rarely received adequate attention, and it must be judged by standards different from those applied to imaginative creations. Fiction embodies dreams (that have often in this century proved nightmares), while nonfiction at least pretends to reflect reality. Steinbeck's shift to greater success with nonfiction after the publication of his last novel suggests a change in himself, as well as in the contemporary world and its reading tastes, that requires adequate treatment in a following companion volume about what proved to be Steinbeck's second career.

The biographical chapter in this book will be limited to Steinbeck's career as a fictionist. It is followed by a chapter on his relationship to *modernism*—an increasingly ambiguous omnibus term but the only one useful to facilitate comparisons between Steinbeck's works and his contemporaries'. The fiction is then discussed in the order of its composition, which, especially during the 1930s, was not always the order of its publication. The conclusion will consider Steinbeck's position in the last decade of this century, three decades after his last novel emerged, and speculate briefly about his future prospects, always a risky business.

The biographical material in my previous books about Steinbeck was checked by his longtime agent Elizabeth Otis. Since then much new material has become available with the publication of many of his letters and Jackson J. Benson's biography, which I have generally relied on for information not otherwise specifically credited.

I am greatly indebted to Preston Beyer and Robert DeMott for invaluable assistance in locating ephemeral materials and for the constant encouragement without which this book might never have been completed. I am especially grateful to Roy Simmonds for discussing and criticizing my work in progress and challenging hurried assumptions. His work on Steinbeck's manuscripts has been of inestimable value. We are all, in turn, indebted to Ted Hayashi for his determined efforts to advance Steinbeck studies.

Chronology

1902   John Ernst Steinbeck born Salinas, California, 27 February, son of John Ernst and Olive Hamilton Steinbeck.

1919   Graduates from Salinas High School.

1920   Enrolls as English major at Stanford University, attending intermittently until 1925, when he leaves without a degree.

1925   Sails through Panama Canal to New York City, where he works briefly as a reporter for William Randolph Hearst's morning newspaper, the *American*.

1929   *Cup of Gold* (historical novel).

1930   Marries Carol Henning of San Jose, California, 14 January; becomes lifelong client of New York literary agents Mavis McIntosh and Elizabeth Otis; meets Ed Ricketts in Monterey, California, in October.

1932   *The Pastures of Heaven* (story cycle/novel).

1933   *To a God Unknown* (novel); first two stories of *The Red Pony* cycle in *North American Review*.

1934   "The Murder" selected for O. Henry Prize Stories; mother dies; Pascal Covici becomes lifelong editor.

1935   *Tortilla Flat* (story cycle/novel)—winner of annual Commonwealth Club of California award for best novel by state resident.

1936   *In Dubious Battle* (novel); "The Harvest Gypsies" reports conditions in migrant workers' camps for *San Francisco News;* father dies.

1937   *Of Mice and Men* (novel); play version wins New York Drama Critics' Circle Award; chosen one of the 10 outstanding young men of the year; first trip to Europe.

1938   *The Long Valley* (short stories); moves with Pascal Covici to lifelong publisher, Viking Press.

1939   *The Grapes of Wrath* (novel, wins Pulitzer Prize); elected to National Institute of Arts and Letters.

1940   Visits Gulf of California on marine-life-collecting trip
        with Ed Ricketts, reported in *The Sea of Cortez* (1941);
        The Forgotten Village (film), made in Mexico with
        Herbert Kline; film versions of *The Grapes of Wrath*
        (directed by John Ford) and *Of Mice and Men* (directed
        by Lewis Milestone).

1942   *Bombs Away!* (propaganda novel); *The Moon Is Down*
        (novel and play).

1943   Divorced from Carol Henning; marries Gwyndolyn
        Conger on 29 March; visits European war zone as cor-
        respondent for the New York *Herald Tribune* June to
        October.

1944   Son Thom born 2 August; asks that his name be
        removed as scriptwriter for Alfred Hitchcock's film
        Lifeboat.

1945   *Cannery Row* (novel); "The Pearl of the World" in
        Woman's Home Companion.

1946   Son John IV born 12 June.

1947   *The Pearl* (novel with film versions in English and
        Spanish); *The Wayward Bus* (novel); visits Soviet Union
        with photographer Robert Capa.

1948   Divorced from Gwyndolyn Conger; Ed Ricketts killed
        in accident; *A Russian Journal* (travel report); elected to
        American Academy of Arts and Letters.

1949   *The Red Pony* (film, directed by Lewis Milestone from
        script by Steinbeck).

1950   *Burning Bright* (novel and play); filmscript for Elia
        Kazan's *Viva Zapata!;* marries Elaine Scott, 29
        December.

1952   *East of Eden* (novel).

1954   Family summers in Paris; *Sweet Thursday* (novel).

1955   Rodgers and Hammerstein musical *Pipe Dream* based
        on *Sweet Thursday;* buys house in Sag Harbor on Long
        Island; Elia Kazan films *East of Eden* (filmscript by Paul
        Osborn) with James Dean.

1957   *The Short Reign of Pippin IV* (novel).

1961   *The Winter of Our Discontent* (novel).

1962   Nobel Prize in literature; *Travels with Charley in Search of America* (report of trip in autumn 1960).

1963   Tour of Europe with Edward Albee under Department of State's cultural exchange program.

1964   Presented Presidential Medal of Freedom by Lyndon B. Johnson.

1965   Begins series of "Letters to Alicia" in Long Island *Newsday* in November.

1966   *America and Americans* (text to accompany photographs of diverse aspects of the United States).

1968   Dies in New York City, 20 December; *Steinbeck Quarterly* begins publication

1969   *Journal of a Novel: The "East of Eden" Letters* (diary kept during writing of the novel on Nantucket, 1952).

1974   Boyhood home at Central Avenue and Stone Street, Salinas, California, opens as a museum on what would have been his seventy-second birthday.

1975   *Steinbeck: A Life in Letters,* edited by Elaine Steinbeck and Robert Walsten (selected correspondence).

1976   *The Acts of King Arthur and His Noble Knights* (unfinished, edited by Horton Chase).

1979   U.S. commemorative stamp issued on what would have been his seventy-seventh birthday.

1984   *The True Adventures of John Steinbeck, Writer* (biography), by Jackson J. Benson; pictured on half-ounce gold medal issued by U.S. government.

1989   *Working Days: The Journal of "The Grapes of Wrath,"* edited by Robert DeMott (diary kept during writing of the novel in 1938, published on its fiftieth anniversary).

1991   Frank Galati's Steppenwolf Theater dramatization of *The Grapes of Wrath* wins New York Drama Critics' Circle Award for best play of the season.

1992   Gary Sinise directs and stars in (with John Malkovich) a film version of *Of Mice and Men;* Nantucket conference on "Steinbeck and The Environment."

Chapter One
The Making and Unmaking of a Novelist

If the necessity of telling stories and the gift of telling them memorably are innate, we have not yet learned to divine and respect the sign that an individual is driven by them. They are certainly not a common inheritance of either those who revile all storytelling as time-wasting lies or those who delight in the joys and terrors conjured up by word-magicians and honor them. Whatever natural or supernal forces, however, obsess one with the crafting of fictions, they certainly set their mark on John Ernst Steinbeck, born 27 February 1902 in Salinas, county seat and market center of California's richest valley, urging him through tribulation to triumph and back.[1]

A Native Son Learns "You Can't Go Home Again"

Although Steinbeck's family wanted him to become a lawyer,[2] he apparently set his mind on becoming a professional writer when he was passing through puberty at the age of 15.[3] One cannot understand his subsequent career without appreciating that this was an extraordinary decision for an undistinguished member of a high school class of 24 in a rural community of 2,500 in a generally anti-intellectual society profoundly suspicious of tendencies toward the "metaphysical," to which Steinbeck confessed to a friend in 1933 he was "always prone" (*Life*, 88). In an unsophisticated community, a young person's conjuring up fantasies for friends' entertainment was no doubt viewed indulgently as a harmless pastime before one took up life's serious duties. Steinbeck might have been pressured toward more "healthful" activities had anyone foreseen the bad publicity that he would give his birthplace internationally before it recognized his value—as most prominent American writers' home regions eventually have done—in attracting well-heeled tourists.

A dissatisfaction with the psychic state of his neighbors could have been detected in this mutant who had been motivated by "mental strife" (though he never used this phrase or acknowledged Blakean influences)[4] from his very early years when he did find in Malory's *Morte d'Arthur* "his secret language" (Benson, 21). The young Steinbeck both benefited and suffered from growing up in a region still living in the afterglow of the frontier experience he dramatized powerfully in "The Leader of the People." Here the idea of being "fenced in" was abhorred by an undisciplined community rejecting heavily regimented conformity, while individuals like Steinbeck were still enchanted by the untrammeled opportunities of a legendary past. A Salinas still in transition from wilderness to wasteland could sustain those who could flourish only in a zone where survival on one's own terms is not constantly threatened by too many—or too few—"civilized" influences.

He received little encouragement but needed little. Between sessions of reading tales and poems to neighborhood children in the family basement or attic, he became largely a recluse. His choosing to spend most of his time in his bedroom writing was resented but tolerated. He did insist on reading regularly to a neighborhood housewife who did not really like either him or his pretentious vocabulary, but when he did send stories to magazines they could not return them, because he was too shy to include his name or address (Benson, 27).

He was never principally concerned, however, with responses to his work. After he had published three novels that attracted little attention, he told another aspiring young writer, who complained that his agent wanted to alter his work, "Don't you realize that you're the one who should be pleased—that you're writing solely for yourself?" (Benson, 284).

He did win enthusiastic praise from one high school composition teacher, who held his work up as a model for others; beyond that he served as an associate editor of the yearbook and senior class president for a semester. When questioned later, however, his classmates did not remember him well.

He also did seek advice after a fashion when he yielded to his parents' pleading and enrolled at Stanford University as an English major, "almost frantically unenthusiastic" (*Life,* 151). He attended only six semesters, off and on between fall 1919 and spring 1925, taking only courses that interested him and frequently not completing them. He never received a degree. One teacher, however, did involve him in his work—Edith Ronald Mirrielees, a short story writer and demanding instructor, who thought that his work should be published, though she never gave him higher than a B. Jackson Benson points out that

Steinbeck was "one of the very few important writers of his generation to receive a significant amount of training in a college creative-writing program" (Benson, 55) and attributes to Mirrielees's influence the development of "a critical consciousness" that gave Steinbeck the self-discipline to develop the style that later won him fame. Steinbeck wrote a preface for Mirrielees's textbook *Story Writing* in 1962, ironically just as he finished his own career as a publishing fictionist.

This career began with two stories published in the *Stanford Spectator* in February and June 1924, stories Benson describes as already exhibiting the tendency toward romantic fantasy that dominates Steinbeck's earliest published novels, developed from work begun at college. Five years were to elapse between these stories and the publication in August 1929 of *Cup of Gold,* though some short stories still survive from the intervening years, and one that Steinbeck never acknowledged appeared as the work of "John Stern" in an obscure *Smoker's Companion* ("The Gifts of Iban," March 1927). Another that began as a bawdy poem in college finally appeared as "Saint Katy the Virgin" in *The Long Valley* in 1938.

These were difficult years, though not Steinbeck's most difficult. In 1925, after leaving college for good, he was tempted to move to the booming East, sailing from San Francisco through the Panama Canal to New York, becoming acquainted en route with the Caribbean regions that would be the setting for his first published novel. After a brother-in-law got him a tough job as a manual laborer on a new Madison Square Garden (long since replaced), an influential maternal uncle helped him get a job as a reporter for William Randolph Hearst's morning newspaper, the *American,* at $25 a week. Had he succeeded there, he might have embarked much earlier on what would become his principal work late in his career, but he proved temperamentally unsuited to the 1920s "go-getter" journalism satirized in Ben Hecht and Charles MacArthur's popular play *The Front Page* (1928). He returned to California to spend several years in seclusion, working as a winter caretaker at vacation homes around Lake Tahoe, where he could devote himself to the lonely craft of becoming a creative writer.

He spent much of this time trying to turn one of the short stories that he had written in college, "The Lady in Infra-Red," into the swashbuckling tale of seventeenth-century Welsh pirate Henry Morgan that finally became the novel *Cup of Gold* and trying to develop a play, "The Green Lady," which he had taken over from his college friend Webster Street, into the novel that finally emerged, after many transformations, as *To a God Unknown.*

He finally placed *Cup of Gold* with the Robert McBride Company in New York, a firm that had earlier rejected a collection of his short stories, and he was able to live comfortably for a brief time on its earnings. This breakthrough had come, however, just two months before the stock market crash in 1929; the publisher went bankrupt and sold only 1,533 copies before having to remainder the rest.[5] Steinbeck published nothing more until 1933.

During the intervening years three other experiences greatly changed his life. On 14 January 1930 he was married for the first time, to Carol Henning from San Jose, California, whom he had met during the summer of 1928 while working at the Tahoe City Fish Hatchery; in October he met Ed Ricketts, operator of the Western Biological Laboratory on Cannery Row in Monterey, who was to become a principal influence on his thinking and writing until the end of World War II; and about the same time he was recommended to the New York literary agency founded in 1928 by Mavis McIntosh and Elizabeth Otis, who early in 1931 became his agents for the rest of his life. (Before that he had imposed the burden of representing him in New York on a college friend, Ted Miller.)

During 1930 he was floundering through some disappointing experiments—"Dissonant Symphony," a psychological novel that he never finished and apparently destroyed, and "Murder at Full Moon," a conventional detective tale that he wrote in nine days and entered in a contest sponsored by Scribners, the publishers of Hemingway, Fitzgerald, and Thomas Wolfe. He also pushed ahead *To a God Unknown* until he was diverted in 1931 by some stories that Beth Ingels, Carol's new partner in an advertising agency, told about a little valley in the hills west of Salinas, called Corral de Tierra. He fashioned these—with additions from other sources and a prologue and epilogue he devised—into a frame novel, *The Pastures of Heaven,* incorporating 10 episodes about the malign influence of a family named Munroe in an idyllic pastoral community. Although his agents were at first discouraging about the prospects for what appeared to be a collection of short stories by an unknown writer, they surprisingly found a publisher early in 1932. Steinbeck had staked out for himself in the valleys and mountains and on the rocky coast of his beautiful native region a locale that was to become for him what Yoknapatawpha County, Mississippi, was becoming for William Faulkner.

Like his first novel, the book unfortunately had to be remaindered when its publishers went bankrupt before publicizing it, but two years later it would fortuitously supply the hitherto missing connection that would skyrocket him into the front rank of American novelists. In the meantime he had returned to a further rewriting of *To a God Unknown*. While engaged in this troublesome transformation, he was inspired to one of those remarkable gestures that would incapacitate most people but that several times liberated him from what might have become embarrassing detritus from an abandoned past. With the man who would become the famous student of mythology Joseph Campbell, who had moved in next door to Ed Ricketts's home, witnessing, Steinbeck "burned a pile of stories a foot and a half high. At least sixty or seventy and all waste in a way," as he wrote his friend George Albee (Benson, 252). Perhaps he should have added the *God Unknown* accumulation to the conflagration and gotten on with the scenes that would make him famous for *Tortilla Flat*.

He finally completed the much-worked-over metaphysical tract for a long supportive New York publisher-editor, Robert Ballou, who, although he went bankrupt sponsoring ventures like this one, then turned down *Tortilla Flat* for another publisher that he was advising. "This has been a very bad year all around for us," Steinbeck wrote college friend and aspiring novelist Carl Wilhelmson in 1933 (*Life*, 86). He and Carol were desperately short of money and had not been able to settle down in Southern California. When Steinbeck's mother became grievously ill, they were obliged to spend many months in Pacific Grove caring for her and for his overworked father, who was also failing.

During this period of trying to alternate snatches of writing with caring for the dying, he hit upon one of his greatest creations, which, he wrote George Albee, was "more being written for discipline than for any other reason," a simple story about a boy who is given a colt, wherein Steinbeck attempts "to make the reader create the boy's mind for himself" (*Life,* 71). This became the starting point of *The Red Pony* cycle, and Steinbeck first broke through into the prestigious eastern journals when this story, "The Gift," and a second about Jody Tiflin, "The Great Mountains," were purchased by the *North American Review* in 1933.

The discovery that was to be most important in rescuing Steinbeck from the remainder bins resulted from a chance conversation in Chicago's Argus Book Shop late in 1934. During this conversation the store's proprietor, Ben Abramson, who had become an enthusiastic Steinbeck supporter, pressed upon publisher Pascal Covici, visiting from New York, copies of Steinbeck's remaindered novels, which he had bought up. Covici had not heard of Steinbeck before, but he sat up all night reading *The Pastures of Heaven* and then phoned Robert Ballou to see whether Steinbeck might be circulating a new manuscript. Ballou told him about *Tortilla Flat,* which he had found disappointing, and put Covici in touch with Steinbeck's agent. Two weeks after a fifth publisher rejected the book, Covici offered to publish it on favorable terms, take an option on future manuscripts, and reissue the earlier novels when commercially feasible (Benson, 313–14). Ironically, *Tortilla Flat* was published just five days after Steinbeck's father died. A further irony has led Jackson Benson to observe appropriately that it was a book "written rather quickly and casually and published almost by accident . . . that raised [Steinbeck] out of obscurity" (Benson, 276). The book put Steinbeck on best-seller lists and won the annual award of the Commonwealth Club of California for the best novel by a state resident. Steinbeck's Mexican-American *paisanos* living marginally in a wooded area on the edge of Monterey delighted readers seeking diverting relief from the Great Depression that they found also in James Thurber's *My Life and Hard Times* and George S. Kaufman and Moss Hart's play *You Can't Take It with You.*

Pascal Covici remained Steinbeck's editor for the rest of their lives, though with a supreme irony this partnership was almost destroyed at its outset by Steinbeck's first submission under his new contract. When Covici accepted *Tortilla Flat,* Steinbeck had already completed *In Dubious Battle,* a project that had started out as a kind of diary of a strike organizer based on interviews but that Steinbeck's agent Mavis McIntosh urged he turn into a novel instead. Covici was out of town promoting *Tortilla Flat* when it arrived at his office, and it fell into the hands of one of his editors, who rejected it because of deviations from the Communist party line. Steinbeck was furious about being charged with ideological incorrectness by some "cocktail circuit" leftist in New York, when he had tried to write an unbiased story based on the experiences of strike organizer Pat Chambers in the field (Benson, 297–98). Since the reception of *Tortilla Flat* had made Steinbeck a "hot property," other publishers began bidding for the novel. When Covici returned and found that his contract had been invalidated, he became infuriated, fired the intrusive editor, and apologized profusely to Steinbeck, who finally decided that he would prefer to stay with Covici. In August the publisher visited John and Carol in California to present personally the first royalty check for *Tortilla Flat,* which allowed them at last to carry out a long-cherished plan to visit Mexico.

Steinbeck found, however, that he could not work there. By Christmas the couple were back in Pacific Grove, after a detour through

New York to sign a contract for the film rights to *Tortilla Flat,* for which Paramount paid $4,000, the most he had ever received in one lump (Benson, 323). Although the film would not be made for another seven years—and then a different producer—the Steinbecks felt financially secure for the first time.

Steinbeck learned, however, that he was not going to enjoy celebrity. He despised publicity and wrote his agents that popularity "has ruined everyone I know" (Benson, 318). "I guess there is no worse thing for a writer than to get an idea his work is important," he wrote Ben Abramson, whom he also advised that he was working on a book for children, "a little study in humility" (Benson, 325).

First titled simply "Something That Happened," *Of Mice and Men* turned out certainly not to be something for children, although the principal characters displayed a childlike innocence (George and Lennie) or a childish thoughtlessness (Curley and his wife). It did prove, however, to be one of Steinbeck's most successful experiments—a novelette that could be turned almost directly into a stage play. There had been a serious setback one night in May when a new setter puppy destroyed about half the manuscript, but Steinbeck was able to reconstruct it and complete the book in August (Benson, 330).[6] Meanwhile Covici had fulfilled his promise to reissue Steinbeck's early novels.

Steinbeck then returned for the first time in more than a decade to reporting, but this time he did so not as an unknown legman in highly competitive New York City but as an award-winning observer of the California scene. The *San Francisco News* prevailed on him to visit the state's farms at harvest time and report the conditions of the migrant laborers. On this trip he met Tom Collins, the manager of Weedpatch, the Arvin Sanitary Camp in the San Joaquin Valley, and discovered the subject for the big book he had been hoping to write.

Meanwhile *Of Mice and Men* had gone into production. At first Broadway producers had shown no interest in it, but the novel's selection by the Book-of-the-Month Club in March 1937 ensured an enormous success. When it became a best-seller, both Broadway and Hollywood grew interested. George S. Kaufman, one of the most popular American playwrights of the time, endorsed it; however, before entrepreneur Sam Harris could present it, a version drawn directly from the dialogue in the novel was produced in May by the San Francisco Theater Union.[7] Then before Kaufman could finish his adaptation, the Steinbecks went on their first trip to Europe. They had planned to go first to Ireland but sailed instead directly to Sweden, whence they visited

Denmark and the Soviet Union (though not long enough to form any distinct impressions there).

Back home Steinbeck met with Kaufman and worked out a final playscript, although he somewhat miffed his collaborator by refusing to come east for the premiere, since he was by then too deeply involved in his "big book." The play won the New York Drama Critics' Circle Award for the best of the 1938 season over Thornton Wilder's *Our Town* (which took the Pulitzer Prize), but Jack Kirkland's effort to turn *Tortilla Flat* into the successor to his long-running dramatization of Erskine Caldwell's scandalous *Tobacco Road* was a disastrous failure despite Steinbeck's warnings (see *Life*, 146–50).

The Steinbecks had driven back to California by way of the famous Route 66 that the Dust Bowl migrants traveled; however, Steinbeck did no intensive research en route. His only major fact-finding trip came with Tom Collins, in autumn 1937, and they did not leave California (Benson, 362). His most important trip was made with Red Soule of the Farm Security Administration to observe the flooding around Visalia, which he called "the most heartbreaking thing in the world" (Benson, 370). He would draw on this disaster to provide the powerful climactic chapters of *The Grapes of Wrath*. *Life* magazine commissioned a piece on the flooding but did not publish it when Steinbeck refused to allow his language to be edited.

Writing the "big novel" was to prove the greatest challenge Steinbeck had so far confronted. He wrote several times to his agents that he was working on the novel, but he felt like destroying it, because although he wanted it to be good, he also wanted to write history and didn't "want to be wrong" (Benson, 375). He made several false starts. Immediately after the trip with Tom Collins, he began "The Oklahomans," which, he told a reporter for the San Jose *Mercury-Herald,* would focus on the irrepressible character of the migrants, who, he believed, would profoundly alter the tenor of life in California[8] (as indeed they did, though not in the ways that he then probably supposed).[9] Robert DeMott doubts that he wrote much intended for this book, because "the migrant situation had worsened, and along with it, Steinbeck's capacity for pity and his need for direct involvement had grown" (*Working Days,* xxxvii).

He turned in February to a satire tentatively entitled "L'Affaire Lettuceberg," a "nasty book" not focusing on the migrants but rather attacking the leading citizens of his hometown of Salinas for organizing and directing ignorant vigilantes to break up a lettuce workers' strike (*Working Days,* xxxix). Driving himself mercilessly, he had finished it by May but then felt it was "pretty lousy" (Benson, 375). After further reflection during a month of revising, despite the financial difficulties that Covici was hoping to ease with this already announced publication, Steinbeck made what was certainly the most difficult, dramatic, and consequential decision of a stormy career.

In an often-quoted letter of May 1938, he wrote to his agent Elizabeth Otis, "This book is finished and it is a bad book and I must get rid of it. . . . I would be doing Pat a greater injury by letting him print it than I would by destroying it. . . . My whole work drive has been aimed at making people understand each other and then I deliberately write this book the aim of which is to cause hatred through partial understanding. My father would have called it a smart-alec book" (*Working Days,* x1).

Then, in the same month that he destroyed half a year's painful work, this man who had written in February "I'm tired of living completely tired" (*Working Days,* 6) turned about and began, from an entirely different, dynamic, idealistic viewpoint, a new story that grew into a 200,000-word novel. He not only completed it in five months, by 26 October, but produced the text in the sequence of its publication with only minimal revision.[10] When he produced *The Grapes of Wrath,* Steinbeck had not only a great sense of dedication but also command of a great talent to create and execute a design for achieving his purpose. He managed at the same time he was writing the novel also to keep a diary—only published 50 years after its completion—that allows readers not only to follow the composition of the work but to share his state of mind.

International acclaim and provincial controversy followed this astonishing performance, though he had warned his agents that the work would not be popular (Benson, 388). The novel topped best-seller lists for two years and became the basis for a classic motion picture, which, though not a faithful reproduction of the novel, is distinguished in its own right. Fifty years after its publication, it would be acclaimed again as an award-winning Broadway play. Steinbeck was not to equal this triumph, but few writers have enjoyed even one of its kind. Although there has been much speculation about the reasons why his subsequent career proved anticlimactic, no one has come up with any better answer than Jackson Benson's: "One answer is that what happened was the writing of the novel itself" (Benson, 392). *Working Days,* the journal of this writing, demonstrates that the writer had pushed himself to the limit of his energy and talent. It is hardly possible to repeat such a performance, especially when it has destroyed a reclusive lifestyle and forced one unwillingly into the role of a much-harassed celebrity.

The Pitfalls of Success

The publication of *The Grapes of Wrath* opened a Pandora's box. The fantastically successful book did not come along in time to save Pascal Covici's publishing house. Steinbeck moved to Viking Press with Covici, but they were no longer in untrammeled control of their affairs. Yet if there had been no superiors to whom Covici was answerable, future problems he confronted with Steinbeck might have been even more bothersome when the writer's life began to fall apart. Unable to cope with well-wishers, reporters, those outraged by the novel, those pleading for help, Steinbeck began increasingly to hide and leave his very competent but rather high-handed wife Carol to fend off a deluge of letters, telephone calls, and visitors bearing congratulations, admonitions, threats, and petitions. (A friendly undersheriff, for example, warned Steinbeck not to stay alone in hotel rooms, as "the boys got a rape case set up for you" [*Life*, 187]).

He had been driving himself relentlessly for a decade, during which he had produced six novels—at least three of lasting importance—as well as a number of abandoned starts and a sizable body of short stories (some of which have also become classics of the genre), while caring for dying parents, building homes, and beginning to travel extensively. He was beginning to need an escape from the spotlight, some relaxation that his demanding lifestyle had not provided.

He began to disappear into—of all the untranquil places—Hollywood, where a childhood neighbor, Max Wagner, was a publicist. On one of these trips in June 1939 (only a few months after the release of the novel), Wagner asked a 20-year-old singer, Gwendolyn Conger (who later preferred to be called Gwyndolyn, usually shortened to Gwyn), to take a bowl of soup to console Steinbeck in an apartment where he was following wise advice and shunning publicity. She recalled falling in love with him on the spot (Benson, 403).

Then, on a trip to the film capital in August, Carol stormed out of a party at comedian Robert Benchley's, and John, heeding warnings to avoid public places, left the legendary Garden of Allah Hotel on Sunset Strip and moved to a bachelor apartment. He thought Carol might need medical help and attempted reconciliation. They lived together off and on until he moved east in 1941 and were not divorced until 1943, but the marriage had steadily deteriorated. Even though she accompanied him and Ed Ricketts on a specimen-collecting expedition to the Gulf of California in the spring of 1940, she is never named in the "Log" that he kept during the trip and subsequently published.

The book in which it appears, *Sea of Cortez,* is something that only a writer at the peak of his success could have imposed on indulgent publishers, for it contained many expensive color plates of specimens cataloged from the expedition's haul, though these could—despite Steinbeck's reputation—have interested only the small audience of marine biologists that he hoped to impress. He had reached a point where he was contemplating abandoning novel writing altogether and studying science. (The book today is a prized collectors' piece.)

His scientific aspirations also involved him later in 1940 in another flirtation—filmmaking—that persisted over a decade after he settled back into storytelling. He first saw film, however, as a vehicle for scientific education. He had become interested in the medium when he had met Pare Lorentz, who had during the 1930s created the classical documentary films *The Plow That Broke the Plains* and *The River* for the national Farm Security Administration of the Department of Agriculture to publicize its conservation work. Steinbeck talked to Lorentz again when they met in Hollywood at a time the novelist was exuberant about projected film versions of *The Grapes of Wrath* and *Of Mice and Men,* and in April 1939 he had gone to Chicago for a month to work with Lorentz on *The Fight for Life,* a study of Dr. Paul de Kruif's efforts to reduce infant mortality that Lorentz planned in response to President Roosevelt's request for a film on public health problems.

Lorentz wanted Steinbeck to write voice-over narrative for *The Fight for Life,* but Steinbeck was interested in making a documentary of his own, free from the constraints of government sponsorship (Benson, 450). Although there was no shortage in Hollywood of hopefuls wishing to involve the now famous novelist in their projects, Steinbeck settled on Herbert Kline, widely admired for his work abroad, especially *Lights out in Europe,* about the growing Nazi menace. Kline wanted to follow it up with a film about a Mexican family caught up in revolution, but Steinbeck preferred to focus on the effort to bring modern medicine into a backward area (Benson, 452–53).

The script he devised became a pseudodocumentary film, made in a remote village with nonprofessional actors—the village residents—and dramatizing the fictional account of a young man's saving the community while discovering his own calling. Ed Ricketts joined the scouting expedition to Mexico, but the relationship between the two friends became strained when Ricketts expressed fears that Steinbeck's propagandistic approach might inspire changes in traditional community life that would corrupt the Mexicans.[11] The film, *The Forgotten Village,* took longer to make than Steinbeck had anticipated. MGM studios also refused to let Spencer Tracy deliver the voice-over narrative as he wished, and when the film was ready for release, New York censors objected to scenes of the birth of a baby until, with Eleanor Roosevelt's assistance, the ban was lifted on appeal in 1941.

By that time this beautifully produced film attracted little attention in the wake of the national crisis over the Japanese attack on Pearl Harbor (*Life*, 235–36). One of Steinbeck's most artful works remains too little known.

While he was making trips to Mexico in connection with the film, he was also writing a suite of 25 love poems to Gwyn Conger, although his wife was still unaware of his dalliance. These free-verse strophes can only be charitably described as written in the language and style of a lovesick adolescent, but they unmistakably suggest that one cause of the breakup of his first marriage was his susceptibility to the kind of Arthurian court-ly love that would have been frowned on by his austere family and prob-ably scoffed at by his no-nonsense wife.[12] Perhaps the most public evidence of his attitude toward Carol is his curious dedication of *The Grapes of Wrath* to her, for having "willed" the book. He uses this same verb strikingly in the short story "The White Quail," about a headstrong woman who locks her husband out of her bedroom and who "willed" her garden, an indication of a powerful determination to force things into being even if the process became painful—as Steinbeck records in *Working Days* he frequently found his work becoming.

A change was coming over Steinbeck with respect to self-disciplining taboos he imposed on himself or allowed to be imposed on him. Jackson Benson attributes this quality in Steinbeck during his most productive years to a puritanical sensibility, but his behavior may have been less influenced by *Pilgrim's Progress* than by his early enthusiasm for Arthurian legends about knightly quests like those Jody Tiflin dreams about in *The Red Pony*. The Puritan's conscience is directed by the sense of the duty of the elect in a depraved world; the knight is committed to a quest for the talisman that will make the world whole again. In any event, Steinbeck appears to begin to have doubts about being too self-effacing.

A change manifests itself most precisely in June 1940 when, after returning from his expedition to the Gulf of California with Ed Ricketts and the unacknowledged Carol, he received the news of winning the Pulitzer Prize for *The Grapes of Wrath*. He had been diffident about awards before—never quite sure of how to acknowledge them or what effect they might have on him—but how much popularity does it take to ruin a man, as he had said it surely would? On 24 June he wrote respectfully to President Roosevelt that an immediate policy was needed to face an "imminent crisis" in the Western Hemisphere and that, although the president had probably considered all facets of the situation, "if my observation can be of any use to you, I shall be very glad to speak with you" (*Life*, 206). Naively charming as the message is, this is the voice of someone who has begun to feel that what he has to say might be important. Indeed, the entry of the United States into World War II led him so much to abandon his previous reclusiveness as to lead him into important and often troublesome involvements with a government whose various agencies had the same mixed feelings about him as patriotic role model or dangerous subversive as the general public. By 1944 Steinbeck was providing suggestions to be used in President Roosevelt's campaign for a fourth term.

As Gwyn recalls, in April 1941 Carol finally discovered what was going on, and a confrontation with Gwyn followed. John said, before leaving them alone, "I want you two gals to talk this out, and the one who feels she really wants me the most, gets me" (Benson, 477). Clearly, in this account we are dealing with a monstrous ego that has routed a once dominant superego; however, this change seems too drastic to agree with more objectively observed behavior from the same period. Probably closer to the actual situation is Steinbeck's statement a few days later, in a letter to his agent Mavis McIntosh, "Guess I was pretty close to a complete crack up but probably have passed it now" (Benson, 478). He was probably trying to face an inevitable decision that he wanted to make not with more bravado than he felt but with considerably more self-possession than he had ever felt before the decision to throw out all the work on "L'Affaire Lettuceberg" and pour all his resources into *The Grapes of Wrath.*

He made another critically important decision—one he did not hold to at the time—to leave the West permanently in September 1941. Had he held to that decision, the second phase of his life—after Carol, after Ed Ricketts, after *The Grapes of Wrath*—would probably have begun then. He persuaded Gwyn to go to New York with him. They departed somewhat more hurriedly than they intended when John was invited to a conference in Washington that would prove the source of his next round of frustrations and accomplishments.

He had been summoned to the office of "Wild Bill" Donovan, President Roosevelt's coordinator of information (later head of the Office of Strategic Services or OSS, that would eventually become the nucleus of the CIA). He was asked to meet with the popular anti-Nazi play-wright Robert E. Sherwood (*Idiot's Delight, There Shall Be No Night*), later Roosevelt's biographer, who would head the subordinate Foreign Information Service (forerunner of the U.S. Information Agency), and others from the arts and film industry, such as playwright Thornton Wilder and poet Stephen Vincent Benet, to discuss future activities.

As part of Steinbeck's unpaid services, he resolved to write his second novelette/play, *The Moon Is Down,* about an underground campaign against an invading army. The first version he proposed was to have been set in an American town like Monterey, California, showing that what had happened to the occupied countries of Europe could happen here (as in Sinclair Lewis's controversial 1935 novel, *It Can't Happen Here*). Such an approach was vetoed, Steinbeck recalled, as "an admission that we might be defeated, and this would have a devastating effect on morale" (Benson, 490). Relocated in an unnamed country that Steinbeck always insisted was not Norway, despite a similar geography and a parallel to the traitor Quisling's collaboration with the Germans, it was written quickly and unenthusiastically received by American audiences on irrelevant political grounds, though it was subsequently highly praised by European resistance fighters inspired by copies produced by underground presses and circulated despite threats of death.

The play version was rushed to Broadway in April 1942 and castigat-ed vigorously for not making the villains villainous enough. And although Twentieth Century-Fox paid a then record price for the film rights, the 1943 production, directed by the undistinguished Irving Pichel, was a dreary failure, suffering, as Joseph Millichap, observes from "unrealistic characters, setting, and events," coupled with "uninspired direction and sentimental acting."[13]

Two further film ventures added nothing to Steinbeck's reputation and a great deal to his outraged feeling of being underappreciated. Steinbeck was never, despite changes in other ways, a good team player. He had fought his way to fame as a lonely outsider, and the troubles he had with the film industry were similar to those of other maverick indi-vidualists, such as directors Robert Altman and Sam Peckinpah, when they have not been left to work on their own terms.

He had been prevailed on by Darryl Zanuck, the producer of *The Grapes of Wrath,* to write his first work intended expressly for the com-mercial cinema in response to a request from the U.S. Merchant Marine to make a film praising its work in the face of threats from Nazi submarines. After seeing Alfred Hitchcock's *Lifeboat* (1944), he asked his agents to have his name removed from the film (it was not) because of its drastic departure from his original. The most revealing part of his request, however, was his denunciation of the cynical, elitist director as "one of those incredible English middle class snobs who really and truly despise working people" (*Life*, 267).

There was also talk of filming *Bombs Away!*, a conventional account of the training of a U.S. Air Force bombing crew that President Roosevelt pressured him into writing. It was the first of Steinbeck's works to have the two-dimensional quality of a cartoon strip that he began to turn out under pressure; no one was interested in filming it. He was further annoyed when he wanted to have the royalties from the book given to the air force but found he would have to pay income taxes on them first (Benson, 509). Meanwhile one finally rewarding film venture that interested him—his own treatment of *The Red Pony* stories that Lewis Milestone, who directed *Of Mice and Men,* had wanted to make in 1940—had had to be shelved until after the war.

A fresh start seemed possible, however, when the divorce from Carol became final, in 1943. A few days later, on 29 March, he and Gwyn were married at novelist Lyle Saxon's home in New Orleans's French Quarter. Shortly thereafter Steinbeck was cleared to go overseas and send back reports from the battle zone to the New York *Herald Tribune* for national syndication between June and November; his absence for much of the first year of this new marriage, however, bred problems with the ambitious Gwyn. When he returned shocked and exhausted by the horrors he had seen during the Italian campaign, she recalled that "for one solid year after he came back . . . he had no sense of humor at all" (Benson, 340). Actually, by summer his good spirits had returned when his first son, Thom, was born, on 2 August, just after he finished *Cannery Row,* "a crazy kind of book" (Benson, 553) that he wrote in six weeks as another attempt to take his mind off the war.

The novel was his first real success since *The Grapes of Wrath* six years earlier; Pascal Covici was delighted that advance orders exceeded his expectations by 60 percent (*Life*, 277). Although it was not officially published until January 1945, copies put on sale for the Christmas trade were soon exhausted. Wartime reviewers thought that the book was slight and unsuited to the times, but the public, book clubs, and Hollywood producers—already fed up with the war—were enthusiastic (though no screen version would appear for three decades). Steinbeck's name still had crowd-pleasing appeal when he was writing—as he would for the last time in this memory book—about the Monterey-Salinas area of the depression years that he had put on the literary map.

Smitten by nostalgia himself, Steinbeck made an unfortunate decision to reverse his course and try to settle back in California with his new family as soon as the baby could travel. He bought a historic house in Monterey, where in December 1944 he began work on *The Pearl,* his first novelette/film project. The production in Mexico, however, involved complicated negotiations that delayed the publication of the novel until 1947, to coincide with the release of the film. The narrative was meanwhile published, as "The Pearl of the World" in the Christmas 1945 issue of one of the gushy family monthlies of the period, *Woman's Home Companion.*

Long before that the new year had brought new difficulties when Steinbeck discovered that he was not welcome back in California: former friends were jealous of his success, and neighbors resented his portrayal of the region from *The Pastures of Heaven* to *Cannery Row.* "You see this isn't my country any more," he wrote Covici (Benson, 567). Although his agents and publishers liked plans for *The Pearl,* they were distressed that he hadn't done anything "substantial" for years, a concern that now seems fatuous and probably dangerous to Steinbeck's development, since *Cannery Row* has come to be ranked often as his best work after *The Grapes of Wrath,* while the creaky allegory *The Wayward Bus* is generally passed over with embarrassment.

Steinbeck turned in 1946 to a synopsis for a project he never completed, "The Wizard of Maine." Although he repeatedly made fresh starts, he could never work out a plot, and he turned back to Mexico as the setting for the first attempt at *The Wayward Bus.* He had high hopes for this prophetic vision of postwar society, but his involvements south of the border were beginning to put a strain on domestic ties, especially when he had to spend almost half a year in Mexico trying to move along the filming of *The Pearl,* while Gwyn had to remain in New York after the birth of their second son, John, on 12 June 1946.

Despite the pressures on him, Steinbeck managed to finish the new novel ahead of schedule in October, so that he and Gwyn could leave the boys to sail on a much-needed vacation trip that turned into a triumphal tour of Denmark and Norway, where King Haakon awarded him the Liberty Cross, reserved for resistance fighters, for his inspiring message in *The Moon Is Down.*

The Making of a New Yorker as the Unmaking of a Novelist

His waning self-confidence boosted by a generous welcome from survivors of the wartime underground, Steinbeck tried to put down his American detractors by emerging as the international champion of Manself's inconquerable drive for freedom and dignity. He accepted the challenge of writing a new play/novelette, "The Last Joan," about France's heroic savior Jeanne d'Arc, to be performed by Burgess Meredith and his wife, Paulette Goddard, at Dublin's famed Abbey Theater; after several frustrating starts, however, Steinbeck came to the conclusion that he was doing no good (Benson, 597).

Renewed feelings of depression were strengthened by the reception of *The Wayward Bus*. Originally Steinbeck had intended to write a short story in Spanish, to be published in Mexico, about a Mexican driver of a rattletrap tourist bus negotiating the treacherous mountain roads of central Mexico (Benson, 576), but on 12 July 1946 he had written Covici from Cuernavaca that the tale "is growing to the most ambitious thing I have ever attempted," about "a cosmic bus," with its driver, Juan Chicoy, "all the god the fathers you ever saw driving a six cylinder broken down, battered world through time and space" (*Life*, 284). Then in January 1946 he wrote to his friend Toby Street that he had had to toss out 20,000 words (Benson, 575). For reasons that he never told anyone, he had abandoned the Mexican locale to reset the tale in the United States, where the "part Mexican and part Irish, perhaps fifty year old" Juan Chicoy[14] drives a broken-down, battered old bus across the California coastal range from an allegorical Rebel Corners on the valley highway to San Juan de la Cruz on the coast. The metamorphosis of this work suggests that Steinbeck may have lost confidence in an ability to address a Mexican audience in its own language, as well as that he was being urged to come up with some message for Americans entering on an uncertain postwar future. His name still had drawing power, and the novel rang up stupendous advance sales (*Life*, 296), but it received a mixed reception from reviewers, while subsequent critics have generally gone along with Jackson Benson's dismissal of its cast of characters—a supposed cross-section of the new American era—as among "his least lifelike and convincing" (Benson, 583).

His energies now turned to starting on a "big" California novel, tentatively titled "Salinas Valley," that would tell the story of his family's years in the region. First, however, another commission from the New

York *Herald Tribune* to visit Russia with photographer Robert Capa would again take him away from home and family. They left in June 1947, and although Steinbeck received a hero's welcome in France, he was treated indifferently in the Soviet Union and in the middle of September left Capa to travel home alone through Prague and Budapest. Following the syndication of some articles beginning in January 1948, the journal, beautifully printed and lavishly illustrated, was published in April. But it was not very enthusiastically received by anyone at a time when American-Russian relations were deteriorating.

John also received a cool reception from Gwyn when he got back, as she was getting increasingly annoyed by his extensive travels at a time when he had begun to find the infants a nuisance (Benson, 608). Just as he had fancied he wanted to be back in California, he fancied he wanted a home life with a family, but he did not. And he was apparently utterly unprepared for what followed when, in his mid-forties, struggling to rebuild his reputation, he watched his world collapse. Rather than settle down in New York and try to patch things up with Gwyn, he set off as soon as possible for California to do research for his big novel, expecting her to follow with the kids a month later. She had been smoldering for a long while, however, about his trying to keep her from advancing her own career, and she was involved at this time in writing, with their close friend Nathaniel Benchley, an unnotable play based on Charles Finney's cult fantasy *The Circus of Dr. Lao*.

Steinbeck had planned a collecting expedition to the Queen Charlotte Islands off British Columbia with Ed Ricketts that summer, but when he got back to New York, he found he urgently needed an operation for varicose veins. While he was convalescing, he learned that on 7 May Ricketts, whom he called "the greatest man in the world" (Benson, 615), was dying after his old Packard had been hit by a train. He died before Steinbeck could reach him, but Steinbeck took advantage of the opportunity to burn all his own letters in Ed's files and to "edit" Ed's journals to remove incriminating references to local matrons (Benson, 615). He returned to New York in a state of desperation to find that Gwyn wanted a divorce and refused to surrender his personal possessions, including his working papers. Attempts at reconciliation proved fruitless, and he fled, this time to Mexico, to collect materials for a long-planned film with Elia Kazan on the martyr-president Emiliano Zapata.

He had been involved in Zapata projects since the 1945 trips to Mexico, during which he had agreed with a Mexican company to make a film. This venture was delayed by difficulties with financing. When he discovered in 1948 that the film was unlikely to be made, he broached the idea to Kazan. They discovered that MGM had been contemplating a biopic about Zapata since 1940 and were having a script written for Robert Taylor—then moving from romantic leads to big-budget western—but the project had been scrapped. Kazan and Steinbeck were able to convince Twentieth Century-Fox to take over the rights.[15] Steinbeck started on a script with "great energy" in November 1948, but a year later Fox had to send scriptwriter Jules Buck to help move Steinbeck along. Steinbeck was still laboring over it in summer 1950, when he had a final conference with Kazan. The company had trouble with the Mexican government, and the film had to be shot entirely on the Texas side of the Rio Grande during the spring of 1951 (Millichap, 123). Steinbeck was not involved in the final stages, as he was busy that whole year preparing to write the Salinas Valley story that became *East of Eden*. Covici had been quite upset about the amount of time Steinbeck had spent on the project. As early as April Fool's Day in 1949, he had reminded him that he could have used the time to produce "quite a hefty novel and been much happier for it"[16]

Steinbeck had a great deal on his mind during the time that he seemed to be dragging his feet on both the Zapata and the Salinas Valley projects. After his summer in Mexico in 1948, he had returned to the old family cottage in Pacific Grove, where his parents had died, nearly penniless and with no income in sight until Lewis Milestone's film of *The Red Pony* would at last be released in February 1949. Gwyn had garnisheed all his income and personal property until the divorce settlement was reached. Covici was deeply sympathetic with his plight and reassured him just before Christmas that he would be able to "start all over again," though he could not resist jibing, "Only it is a shame to have pissed away two fortunes in so short a time" (Fensch, 96). About this time Steinbeck was elected (along with Faulkner) to the American Academy of Arts and Letters, although he never occupied his seat "among the fifty stuffy immortals," as he wrote Covici in 1961 (Fensch, 214).

A trip back to New York in 1949 did nothing to improve his disposition, although it did inspire him to write three short stories about his feelings as a father, one of which his agents sold to *Reader's Digest* for some ready cash (Benson, 633). He had begun dating Paulette Goddard, whom he had known as Charlie Chaplin's girlfriend and Burgess Meredith's wife, but it was not long before he had a serious affair going again. He had gone to Hollywood to work on the Zapata script in May and was invited to bring Ava Gardner to dinner at Nunnally and Doris

Johnson's. When Ava could not make it, Ann Sothern (who had just wound up the long-running series of "Maisie" films) substituted. They got along well, and Steinbeck invited her to Pacific Grove for Memorial Day weekend. She brought along film star Zachary Scott's wife, Elaine, as a chaperone, then bowed out. Although Elaine was still married, Steinbeck wrote to his agents to make inquiries about "the Scott girl" as he "kind of fell" for her (*Life,* 356). They began seeing each other secretly during the summer when Steinbeck's sons (now four and two) visited. This reunion inspired one of Steinbeck's worst debacles, another novelette/play, at first called "Everyman," then "In the Forests of the Night," and finally "Burning Bright," the last two from William Blake's poem "The Tiger" in *Songs of Experience.* It tries to put across through a contrived allegory the tear-jerking but somewhat fuzzy sentiment that "every man is father to all children and every child must have all men as his father."[17] When all the book clubs and magazines turned down this offering, Steinbeck attributed the refusals to their being afraid of a "highly moral story" (*Life,* 408). But finally even he, in an unprecedented statement about one of his works, admitted after the failure of the play version that the whole production had been a mistake.[18]

By that time the Scotts' marriage had broken up, despite Zachary's warning that Steinbeck would walk out on Elaine once he knew she was free (Benson, 654). John and Elaine moved to New York and bought a house on Seventy-second Street on the fashionable East Side to be close to the play during its production. After its demise Steinbeck decided at last—much to Covici's relief—to get on with the long-planned big novel about the Salinas Valley.

Work began on 12 February, along with a journal about his daily writing that was kept for Covici. (It is difficult at times to orient the published novel to this account, since it was kept during the writing of the original text, which was substantially cut later.) In mid-June Elaine and the boys accompanied him to a rented house on Nantucket Island, where he worked until mid-September, finishing up the 265,000-word text back in New York early in November.

In July he had chosen the title *East of Eden* (*Life,* 425). Covici must have been fretting all through the year about Steinbeck's sticking to the kind of schedule he had imposed on himself for writing *The Grapes of Wrath,* for the editor insisted on seeing weekly the copy Steinbeck produced, having it typed in New York, and keeping a copy (Benson, 679). He may have established this practice when Steinbeck was writing *Cannery Row* in 1944 at the Viking Press offices, but he made no criticisms until the first draft was completed. When Steinbeck finished, the publishers suggested more cuts than usual, and he did not complete revisions that included cutting 90,000 words until mid-January. He had intended to follow up this book with another, equally long, about the years from 1918 to the present, but he does not seem ever even to have made a start toward this (*Life,* 431).

He was unable to leave on a fiftieth-birthday trip to Europe that would be financed by a series of articles for *Collier's* (a once leading popular weekly magazine that folded in 1957) until mid-March, but he and Elaine remained abroad five months, during which they visited North Africa, Spain, France, Switzerland, Italy, and later England and Ireland, flying back from Paris on 31 August just in time for the publication of the novel.

The response to it was not what Steinbeck had hoped. He had written the Swedish artist Bo Beskow, "This is the book. If it is not good I have fooled myself all the time" (*Life,* 431) His name attracted an advance sale of 100,000, but Covici reported that the Book-of-the-Month Club could not stomach important whorehouse scenes. Steinbeck replied that perhaps the trouble with contemporary writers was that they were "writing for readers instead of ourselves" (Benson, 716).

The ponderous project behind him, he moved to the opposite end of the literary spectrum to play around with turning *Cannery Row* into a musical comedy. When this didn't work, he was persuaded to "do a new plot against the old background" (Benson, 740–41), a scheme that didn't work any better. *Pipe Dream* turned out to be one of the few flops that the team of Richard Rodgers and Oscar Hammerstein II, who had produced such hits as *Oklahoma!* and *The Sound of Music,* turned out. They had also sponsored the disastrous nonmusical *Burning Bright.* Steinbeck wrote to Elia Kazan that they seemed to be "attracted to my kind of writing and . . . temperamentally incapable of doing it" (Benson, 781). The novel *Sweet Thursday* (1954), from which Hammerstein derived the libretto, however, fared no better as an attempt to update a vanished world.

Back in 1953 Steinbeck had sold to the *New York Times Magazine* a lyrical tribute to his belated romance with the big city, "Making of a New Yorker." But by 1954 he was so fed up with the paranoid atmosphere generated by Senator Joseph McCarthy's witch-hunting that had entrapped such friends of his as Elia Kazan and Arthur Miller that he thought about moving, like the expatriates of the 1920s and more recent writers like Richard Wright and James Baldwin, to Paris. He did settle down there for six months, renting a five-story house at 1 Avenue Marigny, across from the Presidential Palace, that had once been the servants' quarters for the Rothschild mansion next door. He had come a long way from the former Methodist summer camp meeting at Pacific Grove. Elaine had gradually socialized him, but he still disliked the spotlight.

They were brought back to New York, however, where John did enjoy having his own table at the 21 Club, a celebrity hangout on Manhattan's Fifty-second Street, to try to help out in salvaging *Pipe Dream,* though little attention was paid to his suggestions. He was pleased in March 1955 with the film, starring James Dean, that Elia Kazan had made from the last section of *East of Eden.* "I didn't have anything to do with it. Maybe that's why. It might be one of the best films I ever saw," he wrote a friend in California (Benson, 773).

Then he became actively involved in American politics in 1956, the year most important to the shaping of the final decade of his life. Returning to the United States in 1954 on the ill-starred Italian liner *Andrea Doria,* he had met Mark Ethridge, editor of Louisville, Kentucky's highly respected newspaper the *Courier-Journal,* with whom he now corresponded about a series of syndicated reports. He had never attended a national political party's convention before, and he was excited about the prospect of reporting both of them after finishing *The Short Reign of Pippin IV,* a short satire on French politics that he had hit upon while living in Paris.

He did not actually finish *Pippin* until November, after he had gone on 25 August to Chicago, where the Democratic convention again nominated Adlai Stevenson for president, and then on to San Francisco where the routine Republican gathering at the Cow Palace renominated President Eisenhower and Richard Nixon (whom Steinbeck agreed with Stevenson posed the greatest danger to the country [Benson, 836]). After meeting Stevenson for the first time, he helped write speeches during the campaign, and they became fast friends. During the trip he also visited the scenes of his childhood in California and subsequently worked with William Faulkner and other writers on President Eisenhower's committee for a people-to-people program to inspire international goodwill.

With *Pippin* delivered at last to publishers who had doubts about its sales appeal, he became obsessed with his long-considered plans to produce a modern version of Sir Thomas Malory's *Morte d'Arthur,* his childhood favorite, although his agents and publishers were also skeptical about the market for it. In 1957 he and Elaine went with his sister Mary to Italy, seeking to confirm his theory that Malory had visited there.

Then, in what he later described as a moment of madness (Benson, 818), he decided to go to Tokyo in September with John Dos Passos and John Hersey to attend an international meeting of the International Association of Poets, Playwrights, Editors, Essayists, and Novelists, or PEN, where he discovered he was to make the closing speech of the opening session. The next day he collapsed, but he rallied to do some sightseeing before the end of the visit. In 1958 he was back in England in June, going over questions about Malory with the distinguished medieval scholar Eugene Vinaver.

Meanwhile *Pippin* had appeared in the United States, surprising its publishers by being taken as a Book-of-the-Month Club selection and appearing on best-seller lists. Reviewers found it too bland for good satire, but Steinbeck considered it rather nasty and arcane (Benson, 803). *Arcane* was a well-chosen word, for *Pippin* is the only one of his novels that cannot today be read intelligibly without footnotes, but it is also the only one of his short novels after *Cannery Row* to be genuinely entertaining.

His agents and publishers, who had never been well disposed toward the Malory project, were further distressed in 1958 when Steinbeck began, as a spinoff from it, a "Modern Western," "Don Keehan," which Jackson Benson thinks was probably intended as an updated *Don Quixote* that Steinbeck thought had exciting possibilities as a film directed by Elia Kazan and starring Henry Fonda; in a few weeks, however, he lost interest and abandoned it as "hack work" (Benson, 843). He was back to Malory and off to England again in February 1959 to spend most of the year in Somerset near Bruton, where playwright Robert Bolt (*A Man for All Seasons*) had rented Discove Cottage for him.

After returning to New York in November, he suffered what was apparently a small stroke the Sunday after Thanksgiving and was hospitalized for a week; during this period he wrote Elizabeth Otis that he "hit bottom" (Benson, 657), yet he rallied enough to take his annual winter vacation in the Caribbean and returned the first of March to begin work on what would be his last published novel.

He was very secretive about it but did reveal its Shakespearean title, *The Winter of Our Discontent,* and wrote Frank Loesser that it was "a strange book . . . part Kafka and part Booth Tarkington with a soupsong of me" (*Life,* 666). Actually, it was blown up from an earlier short story, "How Mr. Hogan Robbed a Bank," that had appeared in *Harper's* in 1956. He felt he had been writing too many reminiscences, and he made the action contemporaneous with the time he was writing it, from Easter to the Fourth of July 1960, although the book did not appear until June 1961. He felt that "this little thing has turned into a major thing" (Benson, 880), but neither Elaine, Elizabeth Otis, nor Covici shared his enthusiasm.

Once again, as with *The Pearl,* in expanding a short, cynically amusing fable into a moralizing tract, he had watered down and sentimentalized the original. The most notable thing about the work is that it provided an occasion for Steinbeck's being belatedly chosen for the Nobel Prize in literature for 1962, an honor for which he did not even know he was being considered (Benson, 914), although his name had been mentioned since 1945, when he should most appropriately have received it for *The Grapes of Wrath* and *The Moon Is Down.*

In the meantime, although his wife, editor, and publishers again tried to dissuade him, he had set off on 29 September 1960 on a journey to rediscover America by making a circuit of the country in a curious vehicle of his own devising that updated and comfortized the 1930's migrants' hybrid automobile trucks. The trip would become the subject of *Travels with Charley in Search of America,* a meditative chronicle that would enjoy the biggest sale of any of his books upon its initial publication and that would unexpectedly launch him on a new and once again controversial career at the age of 60.

Holiday magazine began to publish excerpts from this work in progress in May 1961, even before *The Winter of Our Discontent* was published. Meanwhile Steinbeck had been invited to John F. Kennedy's inauguration (at which Robert Frost also appeared, to read a poem). Later Kennedy's widow urged Steinbeck to write her husband's biography, and he became a close associate of Kennedy's successor, Lyndon B. Johnson. This increased involvement in political affairs would lead to much more demanding travel and reporting during his last years, but there would be no more fiction.

He continued to work off and on with the Malory material, but he left his modern version unfinished and unpublished at the time of his death, in 1968. He mentioned in 1961 that he wanted to write a novel about Greece, but it was not heard of again. As late as 1966 he turned aside from Malory to start a long-cherished project of basing a novel on the old children's rhyme about Chicken Little and the falling sky (Benson, 969), but he made no progress on it.

He spent most of his last years addressing a series of newspaper reports on his travels. During the summer of 1965, Harry Guggenheim, the publisher of a Long Island daily, *Newsday,* offered Steinbeck a commission to send reports to the weekend edition that would allow him to write off as business expenses his trip to Europe that winter. He decided to address these to Guggenheim's recently deceased wife, "a great newspaper woman" (Benson, 973). The first series of "Letters to Alicia" was syndicated from November 1965 to the following May. He resumed the reports from December 1966 to May 1967, including accounts of his trip to Vietnam, which received sharp criticism in the United States.

He was scarcely back from his last trip when, on Memorial Day 1967, he was stricken with severe back problems from which he never recovered. During his last year and a half, great physical pain was accompanied by grief when his younger son was arrested for storing marijuana in his Washington, D.C., apartment. On 20 December 1968 John Steinbeck died. At the brief memorial service at St. James Episcopal Church on Madison Avenue, New York, Henry Fonda read Steinbeck's favorite poem, Tennyson's "Ulysses"—like the title character, the writer had "become a name; for always roaming with a hungry heart."

His first 37 years had been an exhausting quest to achieve a professional identity. After this ended in fame far beyond anything he had anticipated or desired, it was perhaps inevitable that the last three decades could only be anticlimactic. When the unfinished text of the modern version of Malory that had long obsessed him was published after his death, it attracted scant attention. In what will perhaps be the definitive statement on this effort, the British critic Roy S. Simmonds observes, "It is a literary tragedy of major proportions that Steinbeck never did complete the project," because of "the pressing need to produce books of a more commercial nature."[19]

Chapter Two
John Steinbeck and Modernism

Undoubtedly, enough traumatic events shattered John Steinbeck's accustomed lifestyle after the writing and publishing of *The Grapes of Wrath* to account for his subsequent fiction failing to match in craftsmanship and passionate intensity the best of his previous work. Such personal problems, however, are not alone enough to explain how, at the apex of his career, he transformed a vitriolically ironic attack on his hometown in "L'Affaire Lettuceberg" into the massive idealistic work he produced with unprecedented speed and control. He had been impelled on a new course that was responsible for his greatest achievement but also ultimately for his artistic undoing. While not everyone would go along with Harold Bloom's assertion that nothing after *The Grapes of Wrath* bears rereading, neither has it been convincingly argued that anything after *Cannery Row* has added to his reputation.

If arguments about Steinbeck's post–World War II "decline," however, are to be based on anything more than vagaries of personal taste, some basic difference between his substantial works of the two periods must be identified. After all, none of the surviving novelists of recognized distinction before the war matched their most critically acclaimed accomplishments after 1946. William Faulkner's big novel *A Fable* (1954) is rarely ranked with the major contributions to the Yoknapatawpha saga that came to its awesome conclusion in *Go Down, Moses* (1942), and only Hemingway's short fable *The Old Man and the Sea* matches his harrowing chronicle of a lost generation in the stories ending with *For Whom the Bell Tolls*. James T. Farrell and Sinclair Lewis's later works are rarely mentioned or reprinted. A break around the end of World War II in a continuing tradition in American fiction occurred like those earlier around 1860 at the outbreak of the Civil War and just after the turn of the century with the early deaths of Stephen Crane and Frank Norris.

Such declines may be attributable to nothing more than a diminution of the writers' powers—a burning out of the kind that Stephen Crane certainly experienced even before his death. In the only really adequate starting point to be found for a consideration of this aspect of Steinbeck's work, Roy S. Simmonds observes in his generally approbatory *Steinbeck's Literary Achievement* that "style was, in many respects, the principal force unifying Steinbeck's work. When he either lost the ability to reproduce the mature style of the thirties, or deliberately abandoned it, because of his insatiable desire to experiment, his stature as a writer became sadly but inevitably diminished."[1] If for some reason he had simply lost his ability, the problem becomes one for the psychologists, and one can consider the work of the two periods only in isolation from each other, concluding that whatever happened, it was too bad. The way Simmonds structures his statement, however, with the greater emphasis on the second alternative, suggests he is not satisfied with such a dismissal. The possibility of "deliberate abandonment" at least merits investigation that may reveal that a stylistic change was also related to a change in viewpoint.

Evidence that Simmonds does not cite of Steinbeck's conscious concern with stylistic devices to involve readers more actively in his fiction can be found in the correspondence of the secretive author himself— evidence that has come to light only since his death. Writing about *The Red Pony*—one of those rare works that bridge the gap between undemanding books for children and writing that adults can share and that may help win adult readers among sensitive youngsters—Steinbeck observed of the first story in this cycle, "Mawkish in effect, not in method. I saw to that" (Benson, 265). This cryptic statement is illuminated by a letter to fellow writer George Albee: "It is an attempt to make the reader create the boy's mind for himself. An interesting experiment you see if nothing else" (*Life,* 71). What Steinbeck is describing here, long before critics formulated the principle, is what Wayne C. Booth in *The Rhetoric of Fiction* calls the difference between *showing* (presenting a story "without comment, leaving the reader without the guidance of explicit evaluation")[2] and *telling* (introducing direct and authoritative comment, moralizing). The story is about passionate sentiments, but the narration is cool and distanced—Steinbeck saw to that. He had ceased seeing to such things when he wrote *The Pearl,* in which we are taken into Kino's mind only to discover there isn't much there but "songs" the narrator labels explicitly.

The position that Steinbeck deliberately abandoned his earlier style is supported by the evidence that even so late as 1956, when he wrote the short story "How Mr. Hogan Robbed a Bank," he could revert to the noncommittal irony of his mature style of the 1930s ("And that's how Mr. Hogan did it," he concludes)[3] and then abandon it when reworking the materials for inclusion in *The Winter of Our Discontent*. Experiment always did intrigue the restless Steinbeck, and his long career left behind a litter of abandoned projects. In September 1954 he wrote to his agent Elizabeth Otis, "I want to dump my technique, to tear it right down to the ground and to start all over" (*Life*, 497). The important question is, What was abandoned for what?

Some light can be shed on this inquiry through a comparison between Steinbeck's work and a general point of view underlying the work of many of the most acclaimed twentieth-century fiction writers abroad and in the United States.

Although there are now so many definitions of *modernism* that the term has become as nebulous as *romantic* or others that have been used to generalize about artistic tendencies during different historical periods, it remains the most useful—if strictly defined in a narrowly focused context—to describe the diverse works of influential twentieth-century writers that share an underlying concept of the artist's relationship to society.

As usually overviews of cultural movements do not flourish until after the period under scrutiny, historically oriented discussion of modernism did not begin in the United States until after World War II. The distinguished critical historian of romanticism Jacques Barzun raised the matter in 1943 in *Romanticism and the Modern Ego* when he identified "the modern period in its contemporary sense" as "the quarter century since the Armistice"; in his rewriting of the book as *Classic, Romantic, and Modern* in 1960, he observed, " 'Modernism' is just beginning to acquire the tone of the past."[4] His primary interest remained, however, nineteenth-century romanticism, so that he dismissed the recent developments as "an artificial survival of the last phase of romanticism," which he defined as naturalism and finally found alarming, because "it is walking forward with its head turned back in fear and longing," even though it "defines the revolutionary character of our era" (Barzun, 131).

A more dynamic characterization of "The Modern Element in Literature" was forthcoming in 1962 from Barzun's longtime colleague and collaborator Lionel Trilling, whose essay appeared as part of a symposium edited by Stanley Burnshaw.[5] Deliberately appropriating his title from Matthew Arnold's precedent-shattering justification of the study of modern languages and literature at Oxford at the beginning of the end of the classic languages' domination of humanistic studies, Trilling is much more specific and enthusiastic than Barzun about a particular revolutionary character of their era. After observing that Thomas Mann had "once said that all his work could be understood as an effort to free himself from the middle class," Trilling proposes that this effort describes "the chief intention of all modern literature." "I venture to say," he concludes, "that the idea of losing oneself up to the point of self-destruction, of surrendering oneself to an experience without regard to self interest or conventional morality, of escaping wholly from societal bonds, is an 'element' somewhere in the mind of every modern person who dares to think of what Arnold in his unaffected Victorian way called 'the fullness of spiritual perfection.' "[6]

"Escaping wholly from societal bonds" recalls the conclusion of the novel often cited as both the progenitor and the exemplar of the modernist sensibility, James Joyce's *A Portrait of the Artist as a Young Man,* in which Stephen Dedalus vows, "I will not serve that in which I no longer believe, whether it call itself my home, my fatherland, or my church, and I will try to express myself in some mode of life and art as freely as I can and as wholly as I can, using for my defense the only arms I allow myself to use—silence, exile and cunning."

As becomes the founder/editor of a *Journal of Modern Literature,* Maurice Beebe launched its July 1974 issue devoted to the theme "From Modernism to Post-Modernism" by turning Harry Levin's question into a postmortem finding, "What Modernism Was," and listing its four particular features: formalism, an attitude of detachment and noncommitment, the use of myth as an arbitrary means of ordering art, and its great concern with its own creation and composition. But after compiling this list, Beebe adds that these attributes are not uniquely modernistic.

Beebe comes closest to the vital element in the modernist sensibility when he abandons listmaking to agree with Philip Stevick, "Sentimentality and Classic Fiction" that "one could almost define modernism by its irony, its implicit admiration for verbal precision and understatement"[7] (the specific quality particularly sought in literature by the New Critics led by John Crowe Ransom, who dominated American academic literary criticism immediately after World War II).

Irony, however, has also been used in so many ways that it has become almost as vague and useless as the terms *romantic* and *modernist.* Nonetheless, a definition that relates Stevick's statement to Trilling's remark about "escaping wholly from societal bonds" is quoted from Kierkegaard's *Concluding Unscientific Postscript* by Marston LaFrance to provide his focus in *A Reading of Stephen Crane:* "Irony is a synthesis of ethical passion which infinitely accentuates inwardly the person of the individual in relation to the ethical requirement—and of culture, which infinitely abstracts externally from the personal ego, as one finitude among all other finitudes and particularities."[8] An individual is capable of an immeasurably greater ethical commitment (William Blake's "mental strife") than the society—as one force acting on the individual—can tolerate if it is to make the individual conform to its collective aims: hence the individual's dependency on the Joycean silence, exile, and cunning to achieve self-realization. The "ironic vision," Marston LaFrance thus maintains, requires "a perception of awareness of a double realm of values" where a different sort of mind [he suggests the social reformer Hamlin Garland, in contrast to the self-realizing Stephen Crane] perceives only a single realm."

Now this kind of ironic double vision did not spring into being in the dying days of nineteenth-century romanticism. Melville and Mark Twain, among other writers, possessed it, but their most passionate internal ethical quests were rejected by middle-class conformists. A different literature of cultural assimilation dominated the Republic—most precisely specified by William Dean Howells's pronouncements in 1891 on the role of the novelist in American society: "He can no longer expect to be received on the ground of entertainment only; he assumes a higher function, something like that of a physician or priest, and [readers] expect him to be bound by laws as sacred as those of such professions. They hold him solemnly pledged not to betray them or abuse their confidence" (*Criticism and Fiction,* chapter 24). Howells earned, through his work as writer and editor of leading literary magazines, as well as by organizing establishments like the American Academy of Arts and Letters, the title of "Dean of American Letters." No one of recognized artistic stature since the turn of the century has claimed or even aspired to such a title. Howells's vision was of the writer as an accepted, respected member of society, engaged with other professionals in improving the bodies, minds, and souls of a law-abiding community. With his preference for fiction that treated "the smiling aspects of life," he did not guess how much an authoritarian society might wish to extract from the personal ego.

After the turn of the century, this kind of "Victorian compromise" was to give way to the ironic vision of writers like Willa Cather and Edith Wharton, Ernest Hemingway and F. Scott Fitzgerald, as, like James Joyce, these writers became increasingly alienated from their native culture and sought self-realization in exile. This vision prevailed in American letters, despite frequent announcements that the modernist sensibility was giving way to something that proved to be only a more extreme version of it, until in the mid-1970s it was to culminate in Thomas Pynchon's *Gravity's Rainbow,* Kurt Vonnegut's *Breakfast of Champions,* and the Terry Southern/Stanley Kubrick film *Dr. Strangelove.*

Against this background we can look at the way in which Steinbeck's work presents a changing relationship to the dominant sensibility. This program demands caution because after his earliest publications Steinbeck became as wary as a wild beast of influences and particularly resisted following fashionable trends. If similarities and differences are to be discerned between his works and those of his contemporaries, they should be regarded not as crowd-pleasing but as flowing with a current or moving against it because of an "inward ethical passion" that accentuated his individual perception of the ethical requirement.

Steinbeck admitted that his first novel, *Cup of Gold* (probably like other apprentice works that he destroyed), was influenced by Donn-Byrne (the now forgotten author of *Messer Marco Polo* [1921]) and James Branch Cabell (author of the once sensational *Jurgen* and other pseudomedieval tales), but these writers in an ornate baroque prose of the kind of "debunking" tales that Jacques Barzun denounced as the characteristic mode of the modern ego were hardly representative of the mainstream of modernist alienation. Their style was rather a supercilious affectation that Steinbeck struggled constantly to avoid. He was not always successful, and some critics mistook his decorative touches for sentimentality. He did learn from his dissatisfaction with *Cup of Gold* to eschew models; his mistakes in the future were idiosyncratic—for example, the muddle that became *To a God Unknown.*

With *The Pasture of Heaven* he settled on the landscape and mindscape that were to inspire his significant works between 1931 and 1945. The pattern of this short-story cycle offers a paradigm for the structuring of a modernist ironic fable that could be objected to only as perhaps too emphatically unsubtle, had so many critics not missed its point.

In this and immediately succeeding works, Steinbeck presented an outraged but still defeatist picture of individuals not strong enough to overcome the reductivist force of an insensitive society—victims whose only escape apart from death depends on maintaining private fantasies. The romantic dreamers in the stories told in *Pastures* have all trusted the isolation of their beautiful valley to sustain the illusions on which they have painfully built an unstable security, but all are defeated by the "curse" of a family that violates their sanctuary with fashionable notions and discontents of a consumerist middle class.

Middle-class values take another beating in *Tortilla Flat,* in which the intrusion of property ownership disrupts the laidback lifestyles of the *paisanos,* who live marginally, largely by their wits, in the semiwooded area around Monterey. Coping with civilized burdens proves too much for Danny, who meets his death when he is driven to challenge an unknown foe, and the small community that has grown up around him before the two houses he has inherited have also been destroyed breaks up, with the former participants going their separate ways.

The Red Pony again unfolds against a lyrically beautiful pastoral setting, but at every turn there are death and disappointment. Jody Tiflin, daydreaming of knightly quests, is shocked back into reality by the deaths of beloved horses and a dispossessed old man and by his grandfather's defeat by the dying out of the spirit of "Westering." In these stories, however, the dreams are destroyed not by insensitive people or civilized burdens but—as in Hemingway's *A Farewell to Arms*—by the inability of an indifferent and limited nature to fulfill human dreams.

Two powerful narratives that have proved capable of many readings, *In Dubious Battle* and *Of Mice and Men,* assume new significance when viewed from a modernist perspective. Both confront—with a tough-mindedness later missing in Steinbeck's writing—the defeat of pastoral dreams by the barbarity of modern technological society—the villain that will take its greatest toll and win Steinbeck his greatest laurels in *The Grapes of Wrath.*

In Dubious Battle naively idealistic Jim Nolan is destroyed as much by the radical cause to which he is attracted to find meaning in his life as by its materialistic foes. But even more depressing is the portrayal of Doc Burton, "dreamer, mystic, metaphysician," who—distrustful of all utopian schemes—is striving for complete self-consciousness when he simply disappears because his selfless humanitarian endeavors to help the strikers despite his distrust of their oversimplified program is inconvenient for those who wish only to manipulate others selfishly.

In *Of Mice and Men* dreamers are doomed to defeat—as in *The Red Pony* and short stories like "Flight" and the Tularecito episode in *The Pastures of Heaven*—because of the failure of nature to achieve the perfectibility of which human beings dream. Perhaps the modernist concept of irony can be best summed up by the quotation from Robert Burns that Steinbeck draws on for his title: "The best laid schemes o' Mice an' Men, / Gang aft agley." Steinbeck equals the darkest moments of modernism in Hemingway and Faulkner when George, driven into shooting Lennie, destroys his own dream.

As far as individuals are concerned, *Of Mice and Men* exhausts the possibilities of modernist ironies as Kurt Vonnegut's *Breakfast of Champions* finally does for a whole society bent on self-destruction; still, it seems unlikely that Steinbeck abandoned this extreme defeatist tendency out of a desire not to repeat himself (he could have lapsed into silence, as Salinger would later). *The Grapes of Wrath* represents a drastic change in underlying sensibility that had to be the result of a passionate rejection of his previous conception of the human race's destiny in an indifferent universe.

It is too bad that we will probably never know what conclusion he reached in "L'Affaire Lettuceberg," but his explanation for destroying it suggests that he depicted the middle class losing its last vestiges of decency—like the invaders in *The Moon Is Down*—in their greedy desire to keep their facade of respectability and increase their power over others.

The change of viewpoint that he communicates through chronicling the transformation of the Joads from a self-seeking clan into members of a potential human community is articulated near the end of the novel when Ma Joad tells a neighbor, "Use'ta be the fambly was fust. It ain't so now. It's anybody" and symbolized by the tableau at the end of the novel that was so ferociously attacked by respectable middle-class reviewers.

If *The Grapes of Wrath* were a modernist novel, it would have stopped where *In Dubious Battle* and *Of Mice and Men* do, with the defeat of an innocent but overambitious dreamer; this novel, though, moves beyond the sacrifice of Casy to Tom Joad's vow "I'll be all aroun' in the dark" in his last speech to Ma. There is no assurance of ultimate victory here or at the end of the novel, but there is a replacement of dangerous activism with inspirational encouragement. Whatever vision like St. Paul's memories of the floods around Visalia, California, inspired in Steinbeck, he returned in *The Grapes of Wrath* to his early tendency toward the metaphysical with a perfect complementary reinforcement of word with image. He was not always to be so fortunate in the future. The question he now faced, if this change of heart was permanent—as it proved to be—was, Where did he go from here? *The Grapes of Wrath* ends with the Joads discovering a new sense of mission that may be carried out in various ways, but for Steinbeck and his audience, after modernism what?

The furor over *The Grapes of Wrath* and the subsequent disruptions in Steinbeck's personal life coming along at the same time as World War II

enabled him to avoid a significant confrontation with the problems of
how to have the Tom Joads keep themselves busy on the road but did
lead to his briefly considering giving up fiction for scientific writing (a
genuine alternative for some but not for one with Steinbeck's lifelong
addiction to storytelling). A clue to the future appeared as early as 1941,
when, turning to film as a new creative outlet in *The Forgotten Village,* he
conjured up a rural Mexican teenager who, unlike Jody Tiflin in *The Red
Pony* does not dream of knightly quests in a statically pastoral world but
instead emerges from his primitive village to take on the hard job of
bringing it around to accepting the benefits of modern science. Two
obsessions that will condition Steinbeck's work for years surface with the
brief film: the search for a hero who offers practical benefits, not romantic escapes, and the idea that he will be found in Mexico, for which
Steinbeck had higher hopes than for his native California, because he did
not know it so well.

His problem became that of creating heroes who could be thought
credible in a skeptical age. Mayor Orden in *The Moon Is Down* embodied
the spirit of occupied nations' resistance to the Nazis and won Steinbeck
honors in Europe, but the story proved too equivocal for American
audiences, who wanted their wartime propaganda relentlessly self-
congratulatory, as he later tried to be in *Bombs Away,* one of his shallow-
est works that he turned out reluctantly. *The Moon Is Down* suffered also
because nearly everyone but the underground resistance that Steinbeck
identified with insisted on limiting what he intended as a universal
allegory to a realistic report on a European situation that he could not
present authoritatively.

Disenchanted by the war and his own involvement in it, he turned to
where perhaps at that time the best alternative prospects beckoned for
an artist who did not wish to become again submerged in the angst of
his earlier works that still seemed to many contemporaries the only
response to the times. Working under the same kind of strict discipline
he had adhered to when writing *The Grapes of Wrath,* he adopted an art-
for-art's-sake attitude in *Cannery Row* to create a hero with engagingly
human failings, based on his friend Ed Ricketts, and to portray him transcending the squalid view of the real Monterey in the cosmic ambience
of Gregorian choral music and Hindu love poetry. He was astonishingly
successful in delivering what the soldiers he had met on the war front
had requested—a book that made one forget the war—but Steinbeck
was not temperamentally disposed to remain on such an escapist high.
Cannery Row was a memory book, and writing it had consumed his

memories. He could not find any similarly inspiring vision in his observation of the world around him; what this world needed was clearly a good dose of moralizing, and to administer this he must no longer flow with the present tide but turn back to the generally abandoned Howellsian tradition of the writer with a sacred duty to society. And he must go back to Mexico.

He turned from Cannery Row to Baja California to blow up a folktale he had picked up on his collecting trip there. This became *The Pearl,* a fable in a newly affected poetic prose, which has been widely praised for its portrayal of a rejection of materialism but in which the motivations and behavior of the characters unfortunately appear more like those of the middle-class readers in the United States of the *Woman's Home Companion,* where the story first appeared at Christmastime, than of exploited Mexican pearl fishers.

A more substantial effort came with *The Wayward Bus* (1947), which started out as a work in Spanish with a Mexican setting but was transformed—for reasons never publicly explained—into a case study of what was reputedly a cross-section of postwar American society and its potential savior—Juan Chicoy, a bus driver of Irish-Mexican descent. Steinbeck showed little grasp of the paranoia that had seized an unsophisticated, isolationist American society forced into a world war and reluctant international leadership as a superpower; moreover, he loaded his bus with reincarnations of types from Sinclair Lewis's post–World War I novels, characters that had little relationship to the bigtime operators now commanding the nuclear age.

His failure to deal with an inescapable contemporary angst at this turning point in his career led to a succession of flawed experiments at getting back in touch. *Burning Bright* resorted to pure allegory, with stick figures preaching a then fashionable but not very effective "Brotherhood of Man" doctrine that simply confused audiences with its clumsy attempt to universalize its message. With both *East of Eden* and *Sweet Thursday,* Steinbeck attempted to return to a California scene from which he was now far removed, but the former, his big book about the Salinas Valley, was again overloaded with heavy allegory, as he attempted to mix a fictional parable with bittersweet episodes from his own family history. Again one could extract well-intended messages from the account—but only by suffering oneself in the process of doing so. Started as a libretto for a musical comedy, *Sweet Thursday* could have turned into an ironic elegy for the lost world of *Cannery Row,* yet Steinbeck could not this time find the right note to strike, and the results seemed a superficial and often vulgar attempt to exploit the engaging characters of his earlier work.

With *The Short Reign of Pippin IV* Steinbeck again went abroad to summer in Paris and then satirize French politics, but his knowledge of France was even more superficial than his involvement in Mexico. Though this time he found an appropriate voice, its salutary message about renunciation of power has become so involved with ephemeral contemporary affairs that its significance had become largely incomprehensible.

When Steinbeck decided at last to return to an investigation of the contemporary scene in the United States, he repeated his mistake in *The Pearl* of attempting to water down the tough cynicism of an original fable—this time his own "How Mr. Hogan Robbed a Bank"—to provide a moralizing conclusion that was too upbeat to match the growing unrest generated by minority and countercultural movements in the country while too downbeat to reassure those who preferred to hear that we could return to the good old days.

Steinbeck failed to generate from his post–World War II writings a hero equal to the challenges of the times. This is not a heroic age, and it is unlikely that, even had Steinbeck been able to rise again to the level of compassionate outrage that he felt while writing *The Grapes of Wrath,* he could have inspired it to be one.

His most impressive fictional achievement after World War II was his script for Elia Kazan's *Viva Zapata!,* despite disputes about its historical accuracy. Steinbeck was trying not to write biography but to produce an idealized hero—the man on the white horse who will lead his people from the heavens to find justice on earth. Zapata was the only Steinbeck hero to realize the potential of Tom Joad. In the novelist's quest for a hero for our times, he turned to mythmaking, and in an increasingly visually oriented society myths may be better embodied on film than in print. Ironically, Steinbeck appears to have abandoned film as a medium for his message, because motion pictures can too easily be kept off the market by nervous producers, as *Viva Zapata!* was.

Steinbeck's reputation seems likely to depend on his fiction published between 1932 and 1945, works inspired by a modernist sensibility. He was never able to work out an artistically satisfying alternative. Even the novels that end with a transcendence of modernist defeatism provide no activist models. The ending of *The Grapes of Wrath* is ambiguous. We are not assured that the Joads will survive; what follows is left to the goodwill of readers. Nor are we assured that Mayor Orden's cause will triumph in *The Moon Is Down*; "paying the debt" is also left in readers' hands. *Cannery Row* is an escapist novel that Steinbeck tried to cancel with an ill-advised sequel.

This is not to say that authors should continue, against their own artistic impulses, to write as they have earlier, though some supporters may urge this course. All one can say is that authors should be remembered for their best work, and Steinbeck did his during the disillusioning decades after World War I, before World War II introduced a nuclear age. Speculations about his "decline," though they cannot be avoided, because he persisted beyond his prime, are really beside the point. Whatever may have been the reasons, it appears to have been inevitable. We should be concerned with the legacy he left us, not with what we probably did not miss.

Chapters Three
Two False Starts

Cup of Gold

Readers of *Of Mice and Men* or *The Grapes of Wrath* coming upon Steinbeck's first published novel must feel that surely there is some mistake—this cannot be the same writer who conceived those moving tales of desperate people's struggles for dignity in a land where dreams have died. *Cup of Gold* (1929) whisks readers back three centuries to the Spanish Main, where flamboyant freebooters looted rich cities and pursued legendarily beautiful women, as in Rafael Sabatini's romances about Captain Blood. Steinbeck was not so much influenced by this cosmopolitan best-seller, however, as by the now forgotten Irish-American Donn-Byrne and the once popular cavalier Virginian James Branch Cabell, whose wicked tales of a mythical medieval land of Poictesme still have some cult following. Both wrote exotic tales in an affected style that Steinbeck sought to emulate in what is probably his earliest work to have been commercially published eventually, "Saint Katy the Virgin," an archly sacrilegious tale about a naughty pig who eats her litter but then reforms and is sainted for good works.

Steinbeck had become embarrassed by his tale of the Welsh pirate Sir Henry Morgan by the time it was published, but he was desperate for some income and recognition, and this was the only offering he was able to place, except for a gushy short fantasy, "The Gifts of Iban," that appeared under the pseudonym John Stern in an obscure magazine, *The Smoker's Companion,* in 1927. As early as February 1928, when he had finished *Cup of Gold* and set it aside for reconsideration, he wrote in a rambling, outrageously self-pitying letter to his college friend Carleton Sheffield that on rereading it he found it "no good." He was revising it, however, "out of duty" (*Life,* 10–11). In a calmer but also dejected letter later that year to a Stanford girlfriend, Kate Beswick, he accurately observed that it was "wretchedly structured" and its technique "immature and clumsy" (Benson, 125). When another college friend, Ted Miller, who had been acting as Steinbeck's agent in New York, managed to place the novel, after seven rejections, in January 1929, Steinbeck wrote to A. Grove Day on 12 May that the novel was "an immature experiment" to get "all the autobiographical material (which hounds us until we get it said) out of my system. . . . I have swept away all the Cabellyo-Byrneish preciousness out for good" (Benson, 31, 154). He was determined to avoid conscious imitation thereafter. On 29 October, after the novel's publication, he referred to it as "the Morgan atrocity," though he conceded that it had paid him enough to live in San Francisco in "a good deal of comfort" (Benson, 160). After its publisher went bankrupt and it was remaindered, he wrote Ted Miller in 1932 that he would hate to see it reissued, because "I've outgrown it and it embarrasses me (*Life,* 62), although it remained his only work he thought might make a good movie.

In view of the author's dismissal of this apprentice effort—with which critics have generally agreed,—there is little reason to linger over its shortcomings. But two points need to be stressed early in an account of Steinbeck's career because of their importance in understanding his subsequent writings. As historical romance *Cup of Gold* is of no more importance to later audiences than similar works of the prolific Sabatini or Donn-Byrne, but even in its time it did not succeed as a specimen of this costume genre. As Jackson Benson points out, it never could be read "as a good adventure story," because while Captain Blood and his cohorts were admirable rascals, Steinbeck's Morgan was "ungenerous, self-centered and distant" (Benson, 114–15). Steinbeck never intended to be a crowd-pleaser, and he was unlikely to win fame in popular genres dependent on conventional formulas.

What *Cup of Gold* is generically, despite the fancy dress and pseudo-seventeenth-century conversation, is a modernist tale of alienation and disenchantment; the fictional figure that Henry Morgan most closely resembles is not the swashbuckling Captain Blood but a more recent romantic pirate who lived flamboyantly while secretly preying on a complacently trusting society, F. Scott Fitzgerald's Jay Gatsby. Both Steinbeck's Morgan and Gatsby are poor sons of what Fitzgerald called "shiftless and unsuccessful farm people." Both young men take to sea to make their fortunes. Both get new names—"American Adam" Gatsby invents his; Morgan loots his way to a title. Both become disillusioned opportunists when tricked out of great expectations at the end of apprenticeships, and both resolve not to be duped again. Both seek wealth after being snubbed by fashionable folk, and both embark on a "grain quest," attracted more by the legend than the person of a fabulously beautiful, seemingly unavailable woman. They win their rights to their choices through derring-do in battles, only to find that the real woman is disappointingly different from what they dreamed.

Here the tales part company, as Steinbeck gives the screw another turn. Gatsby remains a naively romantic figure by keeping faith with his dream even though it destroys him and so remains an inspirational figure in an ash-heap world; in contrast, Morgan sells out for personal security and forsakes his quest for material rather than spiritual reward. He learns that one way to cope with the wasteland is to make oneself at home there rather than persisting in what may prove the fatal folly of transcending it.

Such modernist cynicism is stressed especially by an apothegm in which Morgan sums up the worldly wisdom he had acquired during his rise to both power and respectability as a ruler of the world he once looted. When two of the colonial Lieutenant-Governor's former buccaneering cohorts are brought before him, charged with piracy, he sentences them to hang, explaining, that "the Henry Morgan you knew is not the Sir Henry Morgan who sentences you to death. I do not kill ferociously any more, but coldly, and because I have to. . . . Civilization will split up a character, and he who refuses to split goes under."[1] This pronouncement echoes as a leitmotif through all of Steinbeck's fiction, as focal characters who challenge civilization's victimizing them face the choice of either splitting or going under. The great shift underlying Steinbeck's change of sensibility at the turning point of his career occurred when he shifted from ruefully acquiescing in Morgan's cynical dictum to celebrating those who are inspired to transcend its cheerless alternatives.

Although *Cup of Gold* is a cynical, disillusioning tale of the cost of material success characteristic of the 1920s, its principal figure, Morgan, is not its hero. Rather that is Merlin, the ancient Welsh magician who advised King Arthur and who prophesied that Morgan might end up "alone in your greatness and with no friend anywhere" (*Cup,* 28). Just before Morgan dies with his dream of true love unfulfilled and simply vanishes into the darkness, he learns that Merlin is "herding dreams in Avalon" (*Cup,* 269). Like Joyce's Stephen Dedalus, who escapes the "nets" of family, nation, and church to "forge the uncreated conscience of his race," Merlin escapes splitting by civilization by hiding away from it and continuing to make his songs.[2]

Jackson Benson agrees that the novel's underlying theme is an endorsement of the artist's calling, but he soundly objects that Merlin is given so little space that it is "hard to think of him as anything more than a subsidiary aspect of Steinbeck's depiction of a man driven toward a dream impossible to realize" (Benson, 117). The problem arises from the wretched structuring Steinbeck himself complained about. He obscured his own point in his anxiety to get out of his system some of his repulsion by piratically successful "go-getter" types of his own time and produce a work that might appeal to fashionable tastes. His continued feeling that this was his only book that might make a good movie apparently expresses a contempt at that time for audiences' preferences during the silent-movie years. Although he must have felt that he was splitting himself before a civilization that he viewed with distaste, fortunately he realized his mistake even before anyone else pointed it out. He would avoid stylish models in the future and turn out no more cups of fool's gold.

To a God Unknown

His problems with structure, however, were not over. *To a God Unknown* was his third novel to be published, but it is properly considered here with his apprentice work because he had been working on it for a long time before he put aside this increasingly frustrating task to produce his first mature fiction in *The Pastures of Heaven,* which brings together the setting, viewpoints, and techniques with which he would break through to his greatest period. For some reason, however, after writing what he considered a relaxing diversion, he went back to a tale he was developing from a play a friend had abandoned when they were attending college together.

With *To a God Unknown* he did abandon the affected style of Donn-Byrne and Cabell and exotic settings from the romantic past. He turned to the region he had known since childhood, a region about which he would subsequently write his most memorable works, but he had not yet settled on the characters or situations that would release his most passionate power. He was still fascinated, as he had been in his first published novel, with the magical and metaphysical, and he succumbed to a tendency toward allegory—probably acquired from his readings of medieval literature—that was to prove his undoing again in the distant future.

The inspiration for the novel was a play, "The Green Lady," that Webster Street had been trying to write for a creative writing class at Stanford, about a man with an intimate but undefined connection to nature who tries to prevent his daughter from returning to college

because he feels that book-learning will cause her to lose the close connection with the land he values (a fear that may beset a person from
Steinbeck's own postfrontier background and make him wary of academic formalism). When Street had trouble in 1927, however, getting
beyond the first act, Steinbeck took over but also ran again into the
kinds of structural problems that proved the undoing of *Cup of Gold*. In
May 1931 he wrote his new New York agent, "It is out of proportion
because it was thought of as two books" (*Life*, 42). But before he could
write it over, the inspiration for *The Pastures of Heaven* intervened. By the
time he had finished this story-cycle, Street's play had virtually disappeared. The central plot device had become a drought that was threatening the Jolon are a below Big Sur. He had apparently not learned
anything from the writing of *The Pastures of Heaven* that he thought
applicable to what he now considered a parable. Rationalizing his intentions to a friend's mother in November 1933, he explained that "the
overthrow of personal individual character and the use of the Homeric
generalized symbolic character seems to bother critics" (*Life*, 89), as it
continued to do those like Richard Astro, who observed in 1975 that it
was Steinbeck's "most cryptic work," with a true mythical hero.[3] Such
an enigmatic quality was exactly what Steinbeck wished to achieve, for
as he explained to his friend Carleton Sheffield, "From a novel about people, it has become a novel about the world. And you must never tell it.
Let it be found out. . . . [N]one of our fine critics will know what is hap-
pening" (Benson, 260).

This last prophecy proved accurate, but it remains to be demonstrated whether the mysterious "it" is worth finding out. The rambling and
improbable history of a farm family named Wayne that leaves the
exhausted land of Vermont for fairer fields in California hardly repays
summarizing, for it provides no context for a Roman Catholic parish
priest's pronouncement that appears to be what the book has been leading up to: "Thank God this man has no message. Thank God he has no
will to be remembered, to be believed in . . . else there might be a new
Christ here in the West."[4] If the man (Joseph Wayne) has no message,
why all the fuss about him? And if the priest is being satirized as representative of those institutionalists whom civilization has split, why hasn't
the confrontation between him and Joseph Wayne provided the narrative framework?

Such message as is provided comes from another source and seems
unlikely to have wide appeal. Before Joseph Wayne sacrifices himself to
bring the rain back to the parched land, he meets an old man who is the

last person to see the sun sink into the Pacific each night at the exact moment he sacrifices some small animal, looking forward to the supreme moment when "it will be perfect. The sky will be right. The sea will be right. My life will reach a calm level place." When he tries to make up reasons, he knows they aren't true. Wayne breaks in to observe, "These were words to clothe a naked thing, and the thing is ridiculous in clothes" (*God,* 147).

Despite warning Sheffield that the secret must not be told, Steinbeck went on to tell it in the same letter in a manner that suggests a further puzzling connection between himself and his bizarre central character: "Joseph is a giant shouldering his way among the ages, pushing the stars aside to make a passage to god. And this god—that is the thing. When god is reached—will anybody believe it. It really doesn't matter. I believe it and Joseph believes it" (Benson, 260). He also wrote to his publisher Robert O. Ballou that the "god unknown" of the title came from the Vedic hymn "the unknown in this case meaning 'unexplored.'. . . . I want no confusion with the unknown God of St. Paul" (*Life,* 67).

Despite all the mystical trappings, *To a God Unknown* remains an extreme statement of a modernist sensibility's reaction to Henry Morgan's cynical verdict that the character who doesn't split before civilization goes under. Steinbeck will embody this theme again in *Tortilla Flat,* although this time the individual character's "going under" is the salvation of his culture. Steinbeck in his final version was still trying to make something of Webster Street's original concept of a man with an intimate but undefined connection to nature. Intentionally or not, Steinbeck was trying to find a provincial equivalent for T. S. Eliot's fisher king's seeking to bring water to redeem his wasteland. Joseph Wayne does go under, but he saves his land by doing so, for as Steinbeck wills it, civilized materialism is the disease that destroys man's spiritual relationship to the land and sickens both. Steinbeck was finally to make this point unmistakable when he brought it literally down to earth in the tenant farmer's speech in *The Grapes of Wrath:* "If a man owns a little property, that property is him, it's part of him, and it's like him."[5] The priest at the end of *To a God Unknown* was mistaken; Joseph Wayne did have a message. But it was unlikely to win converts, until Steinbeck drove this very earthy message into the ground—as he had begun to do in *The Pastures of Heaven.*

Chapter Four

The Story Cycles

John Steinbeck hit almost accidentally upon the technique that would lead him gradually away from the structural problems he had had with his earliest attempts to move from short stories to novels. The curious thing about this development is that when he did hit upon the technique, he did not immediately recognize its importance. As we approach the first masterworks of his mature years, we must consider what has been so much ignored, to the detriment of both his and his critics' reputations—that Steinbeck was not an intellectual in the sense of being primarily rational rather than emotional. He recognized that he had a lifelong suspicion of intellectuals, with their a priori systems for the management of human affairs, although he would at times dabble in pseudointellectual theories (like that of the phalanx, which will be discussed later, particularly in conjunction with *In Dubious Battle*), and in the long run his work was confused rather than clarified by his greater attraction to Ed Ricketts's eccentric philosophizing than to the warm, sympathetic concern with still undiagnosed sufferings afflicting human relationships that was Ricketts's most ennobling quality.

When Steinbeck made his false starts as a novelist, he was aware that he was more at home composing short stories than longer narratives, but short stories were less financially rewarding at a time when he needed to establish himself with a small audience to support his work. He had not perceived—as had Hemingway and Sherwood Anderson, for example, and especially the modernist role model James Joyce, with his trailblazing *Dubliners*—the rich possibilities in linking a sequence of related but autonomous stories into a longer work that could be enjoyed bit by bit or as a whole. Forrest Ingram, among other theorists, has described this type of work as a "short-story cycle," which he defines as "stories linked to each other in such a way as to maintain a balance between the individuality of each of the stories and the necessities of the larger unit."[1]

On his first experiment with this pattern, however, in *The Pastures of Heaven,* Steinbeck created one of the classics of the genre, with 10 stories brilliantly embodying the disenchanted modernist vision of the ironic difference between the hopeful expectations of naive people and their often cataclysmic results. The great difference between this storycycle and his other early novels is that he was writing in this work from personal experience and observation, not from models provided by other writers, whether contemporary romancers or classical allegorists.

The Pastures of Heaven was inspired early in 1931 by Beth Ingels, Carol Steinbeck's new partner in an advertising agency, who told stories about the people she had lived among as a girl growing up in the small, isolated valley of Corral de Tierra in the hills west of Salinas. Ironically renaming this cove cut off from the rest of the world Las Pasturas del Cielo, Steinbeck explained the concept of the work to his agents:

> The valley was known for years as the happy valley because of the unique harmony which existed among its twenty families. About ten years ago a new family moved in on one of the ranches. They were ordinary people, ill-educated but honest and as kindly as any. . . . But about the Morans there was a flavor of evil. Everyone they came in contact with was injured. Every place they went dissension sprang up. . . .
>
> I am using the following method. The manuscript is made up of stories, each one complete in itself, having its rise, climax and ending. Each story deals with a family or an individual. They are tied together only by the common locality and by the contact with the Morans. (*Life*, 42–43)[2]

Actually, any sensitive reader should be able to grasp—as the writer hopes—the plan and intentions underlying it from the stories themselves. Yet curiously, Steinbeck, whose plans and intentions are too obscure in *Cup of Gold* and *To a God Unknown*, appears to have gone to the other extreme in *The Pastures of Heaven* and made his plan and intentions too obvious for critics who may see themselves in the Morans and need to try to explain away Steinbeck's designs, just as some of his targets in later novels would rant against his portrayals of them and even foment plots against him.

The prologue of this first story cycle explains that the valley was named for the profound impression its unspoiled beauty made around 1776 on a Spanish corporal who was returning to hard labor in captivity some renegade Indians who had abandoned Christianity and sought to return to their pastoral life. He dreamed of returning to the valley, but he died, locked in a barn, of a venereal disease he received, ironically, from an Indian woman.

The epilogue is even more heavy-handedly ironic. A bus-load of tourists peer down into the valley and also dream about the tranquil life it promises if only they could escape their white ambitions. The bus

driver sums up their feelings by remarking, "I always like to look down
there and think how quiet and easy a man could live on a little place,"[3]
before he drives off into the setting sun. By that time, however, the reader knows that distant visions are as deceiving as dreams and that the
enticing valley offers, as Matthew Arnold had written in Dover Beach,
"neither joy, nor love, nor light, / Nor certitude, / nor peace nor help for
pain." Through the intervening 10 stories, one learns the history of the
valley dwellers, who had retreated to this valley with expectations much
like those of the tourists and for a while realized them, until the world
caught up with them.

Linking the stories, as Steinbeck pointed out, is the earlier residents'
contacts with the Munroe family after its arrival. The basic pattern of
these relationships is foreshadowed in a playful conversation at the end
of the second episode between Bert Munroe, father of the clan and T. B.
Allen, the valley storekeeper, which relates the misfortunes that in the
past have befallen the Munroes and those associated with the farm they
have bought. Munroe relates that, because all his business ventures have
turned out badly, he feels he is "under a curse" and now he has bought a
farm that is also "supposed to be under a curse." The shopkeeper then
theorizes, "Maybe your curse and the farm's curse has mated and gone
into a gopher hole like a pair of rattlesnakes. Maybe there'll be a lot of
baby curses crawling around the Pastures the first thing we know"
(*Heaven*, 25).

The shopkeeper speaks for Steinbeck. Though the Munroes flourish
after buying the farm that has been a "curse" to others, the family's presence causes troubles for the other residents of the valley:

1. The false but harmless image of influence that "Shark" Wicks has
fostered is shattered by Bert Munroe's hysterically warning he will have
Wicks arrested for threatening to kill Bert's son Jimmy for unwelcome
attentions to Wicks' daughter.

2. The retarded Tularecito is sent to an asylum because he attacked
Bert Munroe for filling in a hole the boy had been digging; Munroe
became involved in something that was none of his business because he
thought his retarded son had done the digging.

3. Mrs. Van Deventer has to dispose of her demented daughter after
Bert interferes in her affairs by first assuming he must make an uninvit-
ed call on each new family in the valley and then making a thoughtless
promise to help the daughter escape.

4. Mrs. Munroe drives Junius Maltby and his son Robbie back to the
city by publicly forcing new clothes on the boy and making the Maltbys

conscious of how impoverished they appear in the eyes of respectable society.

5. Munroe also drives out the Lopez sisters when he thinks it a "good joke" to insinuate to a pathologically possessive woman that her husband plans to run off with one of them.

6. Molly Morgan, a popular schoolteacher, also runs away when she cannot stand to hear Bert Munroe joking about a drunken hired hand who she fears may be the vanished father she idolized.

7. Ray Banks, a generous man of "meager imagination," is intimidated into giving up his trips to San Quentin to attend executions when Munroe tells him that if he "had any imagination" he "wouldn't go up to see some poor devil get killed" (*Heaven,* 213).

8. Pat Humbert is inspired with the hope of escaping the blighting burdens of his past when he overhears Munroe's daughter casually expressing an interest in his house, but his dreams are crushed when he learns she is not really interested.

9. John Whiteside's hope of continuing a rural dynasty is blasted when his son marries Munroe's daughter, who insists on their moving to town to be near her friends. Then even his mansion is destroyed by a brush fire started at an inopportune time at Bert Munroe's insistence.

In each episode the Munroes have thoughtlessly—though often accidentally, by saying or doing the wrong thing—destroyed a refuge that another person has carefully and often painfully constructed. They are not consciously responsible for these consequences, and they are not, of course, under any kind of supernatural curse. They are a curse to their neighbors because of their insensitivity, yet they persistently push themselves into positions—like Bert's on the school board—in which they affect the lives of others.

Steinbeck takes special pains to plant a clue to his concept of the curse in his epilogue. A prosperous tourist learns that the stone keel of Carmel Mission was built to resist earthquakes but that the plan won't work. A young priest protests, "But it has worked. There have been earthquakes and the mission still stands" (*Heaven,* 290). Like the authoritarian visitor, the Munroes have fixed ideas of what will work, and they are wrong, as they are even about their own younger son, Manfred, when they use the threat of an adenoidal operation as a deterrent when he behave badly, with the consequence that his brain development is arrested by the condition. They are a curse to themselves as well as others.

The stories about the curse are not arranged in a haphazard order; nor are they told chronologically, since schoolteacher Mary Morgan, for example, is mentioned in stories narrated after the one about her leaving the valley. The novelistic character of the work is enhanced by the stories being grouped to create a progression that culminates with the burning of the Whiteside home.

The first three stories, about the Wickses, Tularecito, and the Van Deventers, present pathetic attempts to deal with situations that must eventually be corrected. Bert Munroe in each of these stories is simply sticking his nose into something that is none of his business. He has no charge to interfere with his neighbor's privacy and no ability to handle the situations in which he meddles. In the next three stories, of Junius Maltby, the Lopez sisters, and Mary Morgan, Mrs. Munroe, with her officious do-gooding, and Bert, with his supposedly harmless "joking," drive inoffensive members of the community away altogether by a lack of regard for others' feelings. In the final three stories, the Munroes, in their self-centered insensitivity to others, are not even aware of the possible consequences of ill-considered remarks.

These last stories, particularly, disturb some critics because they do not see how people can be held responsible for the unanticipated consequences of well-intentioned remarks—the stories seem a defense of touchiness. And this is exactly what they are. Steinbeck was a touchy person, and an extreme sensitivity to other people's feelings empowered his most memorable works. This hypersensitivity is often downgraded as sentimentality, but if "civilization" is not based on respect for other people's feelings, one wonders what promise it can provide of a better world.

Further, in *The Pastures of Heaven* Steinbeck does not foresee any possibilities of a better world; the work is a deeply despairing catalog of modernist ironies. Probably this is why many reviewers have been displeased with it. One thing that cannot be disputed about Steinbeck's vision is the correctness of his prophecy about such pastoral refuges. In the epilogue the know-it-all successful businessman among the tourists envisions the valley turned into a subdivision of big houses and golf links. He remarks, "Rich men will live there—men that are tired of working away in town, men that have made their pile and want a quite place to settle down to rest and enjoy themselves" (*Heaven*, 292)—men who, like the Munroes, will bring the curse of the discontents that led them to seek a refuge along with them, as they have to the many such communities that have been developed in recent decades.

Joseph Fontenrose quarrels with the teller rather than the tale when he finds the curse "nothing more than the entry of twentieth-century civilization into the valley. The principal characters could not continue behaving as they had done: their dreams, illusions, patterns, were bound to be shattered on exposure to the contemporary world."[4] Steinbeck could have no objection to this analysis except for the "nothing more" introducing it. Fontenrose is here summarizing what for the author seemed the worst kind of curse that could be visited on a community. Fontenrose appears to find the twentieth century some kind of blessing. He must have been fortunate in his neighbors.

Louis Owens takes a tougher line when he concludes that "the central message here is that there are no Edens, for that is the most American and most dangerous illusion of all"[5] but he spends too much time refuting the possibility of a supernatural curse that is not taken seriously even in the text, and he seems unable to grasp Steinbeck's feelings about the Munroes when he argues that "they may at times benefit the inhabitants of the valley by forcing certain individuals to discard crippling illusions and face reality, harsh though that reality may be" (*Re-vision,* 80). Steinbeck's point, emphasized in his own explanation, is that the Munroes are not deliberately evil people but insensitive, incompetent people who do not know what they are doing and cannot deal with the consequences of their actions, even when they occasionally make others face reality.

Fiction needs to be read in the context of the author's work, especially when, as in the unusual case of *The Pastures of Heaven,* it was sandwiched in between two rewritings of what Steinbeck considered a longer and more important work, one that was almost hysterically committed to the concept of an intimate and mysterious connection between man and nature. *The Pastures of Heaven* was a product of the same mystical sensibility, though its down-to-earth presentation dropped mystical trappings. Owens appears to be reading backward into this early work the postmodernist bourgeois minimalist viewpoint Steinbeck arrived at in *The Winter of Our Discontent*: that one can do nothing but put up with the world as one finds it.

The Pastures of Heaven is an enduring vision from another era. It is part of a genre that reached its popular peak in James Hilton's oversimplified fantasy *Lost Horizon,* with its dream image of a remote Shangri-La, which inspired many in a bleak and hopeless time to push on in pursuit of a probably illusory destination.

The story cycle combines the launching of Steinbeck's bitter and cynical attack on twentieth-century American bourgeois consumerism that would culminate in *Cannery Row* with an underlying glow of the passionate striving to transcend it that would flame out at the end of *The Grapes of Wrath* and *Cannery Row*. It should stand with William Faulkner's *Go Down, Moses* and remind us too that the Munroes function in Steinbeck's fiction as the Snopes family does in Faulkner's, despite great differences between the fading residue of frontier dynamism in California and the bottomed-out decadence of the twentieth-century South. Each writer deals with his community's inability to protect traditions against interlopers and raises a lonely protest against the unfeeling.

The Red Pony

After completing *The Pastures of Heaven* early in 1932, Steinbeck returned to *To a God Unknown,* having decided, he informed his agents on 25 January, to cut it in half and rewrite only the first part, "reserving the last half for some future novel" that was never written (*Life,* 52). He was engaged in this unrewarding labor for another year, until he shipped the manuscript to New York on 11 February 1933 (*Life,* 68). For several weeks after he became responsible for the care of his mother, whom a stroke had left almost totally paralyzed (Benson, 261) he did no further writing, but finally, to discipline himself, he began writing a short story based on memories of his childhood. This story became the first part of his second short story-cycle, which proved to be one of his most memorable works when he finally put it together as *The Red Pony.*

The first two stories, "The Gift" and "The Great Mountains," were responsible for his first important breakthrough into the literary market, for they were accepted in 1933 as his first contributions to a major national literary journal, the *North American Review.* Although the second two stories were written almost immediately afterward, early in 1934, "The Promise" was turned down by the *Review* (probably because of the distressing killing of a mare at the end of the story to save her colt) and did not appear in *Harper's* until 1937, the year in which Pascal Covici insisted on publishing the cycle in an expensive limited edition before including it in *The Long Valley* in 1938. The final story, "The Leader of the People," first appeared in the United States in this collection, but it had already been published in the British journal *Argosy* in 1936. Steinbeck mentioned in a journal a fifth story about the same characters, but Jackson Benson thinks this may never have been written (Benson, 285).

As the cycle stands, there seems scarcely any place for other stories. In this quartet Steinbeck produced a work in which form and content are nearly perfectly integrated as he depicts a naive, daydreaming child developing through a troubling series of maturing experiences into a young man who gives promise of leading the kind of examined life that his immediate forebears have not because of their complete preoccupation with first winning and then taming America's wild frontier. Although not available until after the publication of some of Steinbeck's most important novels, the cycle as a whole needs to be considered as a product of the time of its composition in order to account adequately for its contribution to his artistic development.

While each of the four parts of *The Red Pony* can be read separately and enjoyably, together they tell the tightly knit story of one young person's growth from the selfish ignorance that the Munroe family never overcomes in *The Pastures of Heaven* to a compassionate enlightenment as his experiences teach him to see the world not as he dreams it might be but as it is.

At the beginning of the first story, Jody is a child not only in the sense of being under parental control but also in the sense of being innocent of the knowledge of the disappointments of growing up. He obeys his father unquestioningly, but there are compensations for this dependency, for he believes implicitly in the wisdom of those whom he obeys and lives in a world of certainties.

As the story opens, however, he feels "an uncertainty in the air, a feeling of change and of loss and of the gain of new and unfamiliar things."[6] The first gain is a red pony that his father has bought from a bankrupt traveling show. Owning and caring for the pony enable Jody's first step toward maturity. His schoolmates realize that he is now different, lifted out of equality with them by becoming a horseman in a culture that still clings to the life-style of the vanished frontier.

With maturity comes disillusionment. The story is built around ranchhand Billy Buck's promises to Jody, including a crucial one that he will bring the pony in if it rains on a day that Jody is hesitant to leave it in the corral. If Jody's faith is to be preserved, Billy Buck cannot be wrong, but this time he is, for when it does rain, he has to seek refuge on a neighboring ranch and forgets about the pony. It catches cold, and Billy compounds his fallibility by assuring Jody that it will be all right in the morning. When the pony's condition worsens, Billy does not want to tell Jody the truth but realizes that "he couldn't be wrong three times" (46). Later, when Jody observes that the pony is very sick, Billy thinks a long time about what to say: "He nearly tossed off a careless assurance,

but saved himself in time" (43). But he cannot save the pony. It flees into
a meadow and dies. When buzzards attack the carcass, Jody manages to
grab one of them, which stares at him "impersonal and unafraid and
detached" (50) even as he kills it.

Jody's unimaginative father angrily asks his son if he didn't know that
the buzzard didn't kill the pony. Jody wearily admits knowing, but Billy,
who has started to carry the boy home, turns back furiously on the
father, saying, "Course he knows it. . . . Jesus Christ! man, can't you see
how he'd feel about it?" (50). Jody is practicing displacement, as he has
earlier when he throws a clod at an unoffending but disgustingly healthy
dog when the pony is dying. He has learned that one cannot always hit
back directly at the source of suffering; more important, he has learned
that nature is impersonal, no respecter of human wishes.

As the second story begins, the once naively trusting Jody has become
cruel and callous. He irrationally tortures the long-suffering dog and
kills a thrush. Then he hides the songbird's body to avoid telling the
truth, because "he didn't care about the bird, or its life, but he knew
what the older people would say if they had seen him kill it; he was
ashamed of their potential opinion" (55). He has graduated to that inter-
mediate state between childhood and adulthood when he no longer
respects his elders but still fears their control—that state in which one's
principal guide to conduct is fear of public opinion, one beyond which
many perpetually resentful people never advance.

Like these, Jody shuns responsibility. When an old man approaches
him, asking for help, Jody turns abruptly and runs to the house. The old
man has lived on the land where the ranch now stands, and he has come
home to die. Jody's father, who unsympathetically refuses to let this dispossessed figure from the Mexican era stay, compares him to an old horse
"who ought to be shot" (65). Jody summons up the courage, however, to
speak sympathetically to the old man and learns that his most prized
possession is a rapier he has inherited from his father. The next morning
both the aged visitor and the superannuated horse Easter have disappeared into the great mountains on the horizon that Jody greatly
admires. As the boy thinks of old Gitano, he is filled with "a nameless
sorrow" (72). He has learned that adults are not always to be feared, that
they have their problems, that they become worn-out, unwanted.

"The Promise" opens with Jody's demonstrating his consciousness of
the hurt feelings adults can experience and being treated by them in a
more grown-up manner. His father promises him a colt to replace the
red pony if the boy will take the mare to be bred, earn the stud fee, tend

the mare until she is ready to deliver (nearly a year), and then train the colt. Jody promises and finds himself reduced "to peonage for the whole late spring and summer" (88). Billy Buck will do everything he can to deliver the colt safely but "won't promise anything" (91). Jody endures the kind of ordeal that a medieval squire would have had to go through as a condition of attaining knighthood. In the end tragedy strikes again: something goes wrong with the delivery, and Billy has to kill the mare to save the colt. During these tense moments two traumatic role reversals occur in Jody and Billy Buck's relationship: Jody, who used to obey automatically, refuses to do so until sworn at, and Billy for the first time loses his temper with the boy because of his frustration at the loss of the mare.

Jody has now irreversibly entered the troublesome realm of adult emotions and defeats. He has learned that just as man is fallible, so is nature. The mare has successfully delivered colts before, but this time something beyond remedying has gone wrong. An old life must sometimes be sacrificed, not because it has become useless, as in the previous story, but in order to make a new one possible. Nobody is at fault; the system is just not perfect. Jody has gotten what he wanted but has also learned what one's dreams may cost.

The last story, "The Leader of the People," climaxes the history of Jody's maturing. It is skillfully linked to the preceding one by Jody's first use of the profanity he has picked up from Billy Buck at the end of "The Promise." When he says, "I hope it don't rain until after I kill those damn mice," he looks over his shoulder "to see whether Billy had noticed the mature profanity." But the ranchhand makes no comment (109).

The story is built around a visit from Jody's maternal grandfather, who had once led migrants across the plains during pioneering days. Jody's father does not look forward to the visit, because of the old man's interminable reminiscing about his great experience. "He just goes on and on, and he never changes a word," the father complains, but his wife replies quietly, "That was the big thing in my father's life. He led a wagon train clear across the plains to the coast, and when it was finished, his life was done. It was a big thing to do, but it didn't last long enough" (112).

When the old man arrives, he starts repeating his story. Although Jody listens enthusiastically, confrontation occurs when his father, thinking the grandfather out of earshot, asks with irritation, "Why does he have to tell [his stories] over and over?" (124). This time the old man overhears him and says gently, "An old man doesn't see things sometimes. Maybe you're right. The crossing is finished. Maybe it should be forgotten, now it's done" (125). He goes out to sit on the porch, "looking small and thin and black" (126). Jody joins him as he begins to talk: "I tell these old stories, but they're not what I want to tell. I only know how I want people to feel when I tell them. It wasn't the Indians that were important, nor adventures, nor even getting out here. It was a whole bunch of people made into one big crawling best. And I was the head. It was westering and westering. . . . Then we came down to the sea and it was done. . . . That's what I should be telling instead of stories" (129). The tragedy is not just that "There's a line of old men along the shore hating the ocean because it stopped them" but that "Westering has died out of the people" (130). Jody learns that just as nature is imperfect, it also—like humans—has its limits, wears out, offers no new frontiers. And he also learns something that the imaginative artist finds even more frustrating in his relations with practical-minded men: that experience may be incommunicable, the urges demanding it impossible to share. One who strives to inspire the young seems just a long-winded survivor of a vanished world.

In the last lines of the cycle, Jody shows that he has learned even more. He offers to make the old man a lemonade. When his mother joshes that he wants one for himself, he replies, "No, Ma'am, I don't want one." She starts to say, "Jody! You're sick," but she stops suddenly and helps him (131). Small though his gesture may be, the boy is trying to show compassion through an altruistic action. He has truly matured, achieved his knighthood, since he has learned that the only way to deal with the fallibility and limitations of both men and nature is to try to ease the pain.

Such moralizing is not as obvious in the story-cycle as this explanation makes it appear, because Steinbeck succeeds here in so fusing form and content that the complex message of the narrative is not forced, obtrusive or long-winded. In the depiction of a temperamental child emerging into compassionate maturity by painfully learning through personal experiences about the fallibility of people, the wearing out of people, the unreliability of nature, and the exhaustion of nature, Steinbeck succeeds in doing what Jody's grandfather feels he has failed to do—make people "feel" the way he wishes when he tells his stories.[7]

That Steinbeck had a sense of the universal significance of these haunting recollections of childhood is evident from an unpublished introduction that he wrote in 1964 for the suite of concert music derived by Aaron Copland from his background music for the film version of *The*

Red Pony (1949). Copland had asked the aging Steinbeck if he would write an introduction that could be read at performances of the suite at children's concerts. Steinbeck replied enthusiastically with a "Narration" about 300 words long, which describes a kind of "everyboy" whose experiences are recalled by the suite and who ends up as the kind of everyman Steinbeck had also tried to create in *Burning Bright* as a result of passing through the experience. Copland felt that it was not suitable for children, but Steinbeck did not wish to revise it.[8] It has apparently never been published, but it should be included with every reprinting of the complete *Red Pony* cycle.

Copland's misgivings call attention to the essentially modernist viewpoint permeating this cycle about childhood—vastly different from the fatuousness of much "children's literature." *The Red Pony* is not a happy work; it is essentially a story about "splitting" by civilization, about confronting a series of defeats and learning to handle defeat with dignity. The defeatism of the outlook is embodied in a key exchange between Jody and his grandfather near the end of the cycle, when Jody speculates, "Maybe I could lead the people some day," and the grandfather replies with the last word, "No place to go. . . .But that's not the worst. . . . Westering has died out of the people. Your father is right. It is finished" (130).

Steinbeck made a significant change in the cycle when he drastically reorganized it into a straightforward narrative moving toward a single climax for the film version after World War II,[9] The reorientation provides a striking illustration of a fundamental change in the underlying sensibility informing his works, beginning with *The Grapes of Wrath*. The episode about the old Mexican Gitano's coming home to die is dropped altogether and replaced with some scenes that sketch in Jody's father's decision not to accept an opportunity to move into town and become a shopkeeper but to remain on the ranch, a refusal to be split by middle-class civilization in accord with the conception of some redemptory quality in maintaining an intimate connection with the land. The result of the change is a charming pastoral in which both mare and colt survive, but while the original story cycle is not just a "children's story" but a universal initiation myth, the rewrite is a "children's movie."[10]

Tortilla Flat

Steinbeck had trudged a long trail to a quite different world between his two treatments of *The Red Pony*. He would complete one more story

cycle before turning to his more conventionally novelistic works, a work
that raises the intriguing question of what readers' first impression of
Steinbeck were when he hit the best-seller lists in 1935. Only a handful
would have been aware of him earlier. His first three publishers were
bankrupt, and the novels had been remaindered. It is not really likely
that the cynical costume piece *Cup of Gold* or the cryptically metaphysical *To a God Unknown* would have won many readers, but *The Pastures of
Heaven,* the novel that attracted Pascal Covici to Steinbeck's work, well
promoted, might have won readers attracted to the ironic modernist
vein of Sherwood Anderson's *Winesburg, Ohio* cycle or Sinclair Lewis's
debunking attacks on middle-class midwesterners or H. L. Mencken's
lambasting of the American "booboisie." *Tortilla Flat,* however, won
Steinbeck a following on other grounds and created expectations that
made his major works to follow a series of startling surprises.

Jackson Benson is right in his reflection that "one of the ironies of
[Steinbeck's] career was that this book, written rather quickly and casually and published almost by accident, was the book that raised him out
of obscurity" (Benson, 276). Steinbeck himself did not think much of it.
He wrote his agents in June 1935, "Curious that this second-rate book,
written for relaxation, should cause this fuss. People are actually taking
it seriously" (*Life,* 111).

The novel, however, fared well, going into numerous editions and
even warranting an elaborate and quite expensive for the time new illustrated edition in 1947. But Steinbeck's judgment proves right in the
long run. The story cycle has become embarrassingly dated, and if his
reputation depended on it, he would probably be dismissed, as is
William Saroyan, as a regional local colorist, though some readers wish
he had continued working in this vein. What won him his first substantial audience?

Even though the characters' behavior would scarcely raise an eyebrow
a half-century later, *Tortilla Flat* when it appeared appears was considered not just risqué but shocking, because of the characters' uninhibited
libidos and flagrant disregard for property and propriety. The strict Hays
code had recently been instituted to limit movies to the most decorous,
hands-off boy-meets-girl stories and a procession of pompous, edifying
biographies. The radio was similarly watchhawked to inoffensive jokes
and tear-jerking tales of family crises, so that audiences had to turn to
books for anything that might be considered daring, and even they
might be banned somewhere if their language or situations offended del-
icate sensibilities.

Steinbeck promised to spin tales of the Pacific slopes to rival Erskine Caldwell's wildly popular and widely denounced tales of southern degeneracy along *Tobacco Road*, although Jack Kirkland, who had turned this scandalous novel into Broadway's longest-running hit, found that he could not turn the same trick with Steinbeck's *paisanos*. The escapist appeal of Steinbeck's tales during the depression lay rather with that of George S. Kaufman and Moss Hart's enormously popular 1936 play, *You Can't Take It with You,* and "zany" films like Gregory LaCava's *My Man Godfrey* (also 1936), which enchanted crowds with the message that one did not need money after all to live happily on the margins of society. The *paisano* tales appealed to those fed up with the deprivation of the times.

Steinbeck's subsequent novels came as great shocks to those who read *Tortilla Flat* in the same vein as James Thurber's *My Life and Hard Times* (1933), as mocking the defeatist spirit of the time, though readers might have been alerted as to what to expect had they paid more attention to the cycle's downbeat ending; still, this was a work better taken in parts than as a whole. Like *The Red Pony, Tortilla Flat,* despite comic episodes, is not a happy book. But in this work the characters do not learn to "split," to accept defeat with resignation but compassionate dignity. Danny, at the end of the tales, cannot make the adjustment to the ownership of property that civilization demands, but neither can he return to the wild life in the woods. He can only destroy himself by challenging the "enemy" who is worthy of him.

Jackson Benson treats *Tortilla Flat* as even at the time of its publication a tour de force that only Steinbeck could have gotten away with (Benson, 279), but it does not work today, for what once seemed comforting escapism may appear discomforting exploitation. Steinbeck has been praised for his understanding of the Mexican psyche; nevertheless, at the present distance from his writings one feels that while he displayed much greater tolerance and self-indulgent envy for Monterey's *paisanos* during a trying period in his own life, he understood them little better than most other Californian Anglos. He stressed to Joseph Henry Jackson, a sympathetic reviewer for the *San Francisco Chronicle,* that "those people" in the novel were "very dear" to him; however, such affection does not rule out one's yet being patronizing, as one can be to children, especially if the characters' charm derives from a childlike innocence.

Certainly Steinbeck did not share the views that Frank Norris expressed in 1901 in *The Octopus:* "The Anglo-Saxon spectators round about drew back in disgust, but the hot, degenerated blood of Portuguese, Mexican, and mixed Spanish boiled up in excitement" at the slaughter of jackrabbit that had been rounded up.[11] But it was nearly impossible in the atmosphere of agricultural California to avoid the attitude from which the humor in these stories derives—even if one held it with some wistfulness—that "these people" whom the Anglos had dispossessed could not survive in the new society.

In the 1930s the *paisanos* were viewed at best (many Anglos simply depised them, as they still do) as ingratiating but ineffectual people. The affected style Steinbeck employed in this novel—for the last time until *The Pearl* (actually set in Mexico)—distanced the *paisanos* from the well-meaning but repressed Anglos who made their weary ways through Steinbeck's carnivalesque work; it lent if not credibility a kind of other-worldliness to the story of old Pirate and his saintly dogs and the golden candlestick. Even Steinbeck's insistence on trying to call to the reader's attention parallels between the *paisanos* brotherhood and King Arthur's round table that some critics still have trouble perceiving strikes a condescending note through its implication that the characters are worth attention only because they can be endowed with some mystical significance.

A work whose slender claims the author recognized rested on a whimsical charm has suffered from a now discredited *Norteamericano* view of Latin Americans. Especially during Prohibition, when Tortilla Flat flourished, Anglos' dream of orgiastic living—beyond such capitals of wickedness as New Orleans and Reno—were inspired by legends imported across the Mexican border and especially up from Havana. In 1960 the carnival was still in progress, and it was possible to inflate the marginal figures of the *paisanos* to mythical status to bludgeon satirically respectable middle-class Americans—Camelot had not been temporarily relocated in Washington, D.C., the vast midwestern migration into California had increased fundamentalist Anglo ascendancy, and Mexican "wetbacks" had taken the bottom-rung seasonal jobs that former Okies would reject as they did that humiliating brand itself, while Cuba was just learning that the party was over.

The naive fictional treatment of Latin Americans (or other minorities) as childlike rascals has become offensive to sensitive readers of any origin. The question one must ask is, Could one be comfortable reading *Tortilla Flat* with a mixed classroom of Anglos and Chicanos? In a previous book I argued that early concentration on possible Arthurian parallels in the novel has been the product of "a red herring dragged across

the path by the author himself" that obscured the basically satiric intentions of the novel. What I should have said was that this was an indication that there was less to the novel than meets the eye—that it did not
probe deeply serious issues of human socialization (as Steinbeck's next
novels would) but simply provided carnivalesque escape. Louis Owens
has observed quite soundly that it is "perhaps the most pessimistic of
Steinbeck's works, rivaled in its darkness only by *In Dubious Battle*" (*Re-
Vision,* 177). But we need to go a step further and recall that Lent tradi-
tionally follows Carnival, and, recalling Henry Morgan's dictum in *Cup
of Gold* that "civilization will split up a man, and he who does not split
goes under," observe that Danny chooses to go under rather than split.
There is a difference here, however, from *In Dubious Battle* and the Jim
Casy story in *The Grapes of Wrath.* Danny does not die *for* anything; he
simply self-destructs out of psychopathic self-indulgence. Jim Nolan
goes under, but he does not self-destruct. He dies in an effort to aid a
friend (though he acted too carelessly on what might be a false report)
and a cause he believes in (though its merits may be dubious). There is a
social comment here, though Steinbeck is not taking sides; he is lament-
ing that a talented young person capable of such dedication is wasted by
a thoughtless society. Danny is, furthermore, no Christ figure; there will
be no resurrection after his court disperses, no reincarnation in an inspiring figure like Tom Joad. His death simply brings the story to a macabre
end, beyond which there is nothing. One can enjoy the fun while it lasts
in *Tortilla Flat,* but there is no reason to go back there. The author
proved his own best critic when he described this as a "second rate book,
written for relaxation." One wonders about a society—and its motives—
that awards such a work a prize.

Chapter Five

Travels through the Long Valley

Although a collection of Steinbeck's short stories was not published until 1938, all of the stories in *The Long Valley* had been completed by the middle of 1934, before he started work on *In Dubious Battle*. They therefore are both formally and chronologically most closely related to Steinbeck's story-cycles. To understand the development of these themes and techniques, these stories should be reviewed before any consideration of his first well-constructed long narrative, which is widely regarded as his first important novel.

Except for the four *Red Pony* stories, which are printed in this collection, the stories included do not constitute any kind of connected cycle. Yet if the other stories, except for the very early "Saint Katy the Virgin," were presented in a slightly different order from the present one that seems to follow no particular plan, they might be even more enjoyably read as the record of several stages in the development of a unifying sensibility, although no such possibility has been explored in any of several critical studies devoted exclusively to Steinbeck's short stories. Since all but "Saint Katy" were written during a comparatively brief period— during a year after which Steinbeck would shift from his earlier episodic works and essentially romantic local-color stories to tightly dramatically structured narratives about some of the most urgent problems facing contemporary society—it would not be surprising if concerns underlying and inspiring one story should lead him to related considerations in devising the next.[1]

A plan for slightly rearranging the contents of the volume might suggest how the development of a sensitive observer's experiences lead to the melancholic disenchantment of his youthful romantic enthusiasms. It would have the collection begin instead of end with *The Red Pony* cycle as the record of a sensitive young man's maturing through his experience with the inevitable defeats inflicted by fallible men and nature. Starting the collection with this establishment of the youthful character development of Jody Tiflin leaves questions about what may have become of him.

While Steinbeck makes no connection between Jody and the other stories, the boy grown up could easily have been involved in such incidents in his home country as a participant or witness or collector of local tales such as Steinbeck had used in *The Pastures of Heaven* and *Tortilla Flat*. To link *The Red Pony* with nine of the other stories, the shortest and what seems the least complex and complete, "Breakfast," could be placed between the two groups.

In my first book about Steinbeck I shared a general tendency to dismiss "Breakfast" as an idyllic sketch not because it failed to dramatize a moving situation but because I did not think such an explicit narrative could be misinterpreted. I was wrong. Despite Michael J. Meyers's comment that in the collected stories, "Steinbeck's vision of human life appears as a journey through a long valley, complete with all its paradoxical visions of good and evil" (*Stories*, 33), a most useful insight for reorganizing the contents, he writes that when a migrant family invite the narrator to join them for breakfast and then offer him work, "he *surprisingly* rejects them" (*Stories*, 34; my italics). Meyers also overlooks the significance of the laconic narrator's most personally revealing opening comments—to readers, not to his hosts—that he finds himself recalling this encounter "again and again, each time bringing more detail out of a sunken memory, remembering brings the curious warm pleasure" and his praising at the end, "some element of great beauty there."

The narrator makes it clear from the beginning of his conversation with the unnamed family that he is *not* looking for work picking cotton and repeats at the end, when asked again, "No, I got to go along." There is no indication that he is a migrant, however, and he cannot be carrying any possessions, as he puts his hands in his pockets early in the story. He is a man out for a walk in the early morning who has someplace to stay nearby and something to do in the region. Actually, Jackson Benson identifies "Breakfast" as a transcription of a "very real scene" that came out of Steinbeck's visits with migrant workers while preparing to write *In Dubious Battle* (Benson, 291).

We should not need such biographical information, however, to realize that the importance of the incident lies in the deep impression it makes on the narrator, who could certainly be a grown-up Jody Tiflin—or indeed John Steinbeck. The incident has made such a profound impression because this instance of communal generosity by a family happy at enjoying a moment of prosperity in difficult times is something rare in his experience. If this moment comes to mean so much to him, what must the rest of his adult life have been like? This need remain no rhetorical question, for placing the nine remaining stories in this collection after "Breakfast" could provide a clear and disheartening answer to it. Seen as a record of recollections of a single consciousness, they present an appalling picture of one's encounters in a long valley, whether this is conceived of as a particular feature of the California landscape or as the road one treads through life. Certainly they are the product of the same defeatist modernist literary sensibility as the novels Steinbeck had written during the same years.

Some intriguing efforts have been made to find a more specific theme or observation about human nature unifying the stories. Susan Shillinglaw's opening observation that in "The Chrysanthemums" Steinbeck delineates "the stifling effects of both sexual repression and middle-class complacency" (*Stories,* 1) can be extended to all the stories except "Flight," the most totally objective and distanced of the group, so that it may be the one to which to turn for a first clue to some overall view.

"Flight"

"Flight" is something rare—a totally naturalistic account without editorial comment, of something that happened. Edwin Cady objects that "there really are no naturalists in American literature," because he is unaware of any work of fiction that will adequately and consistently stand for "the naturalist sensibility," which would reduce man "to the merest organism, fighting meaninglessly, at the mercy of chance and force to foredoomed loss."[2] Certainly Steinbeck proved no consistently naturalistic writer, but in "Flight" he met the challenge. It is the only "long valley" story that he was unable to place in a magazine before the publication of the collection, but in the nuclear age it has become a popular anthology piece.

Nineteen-year-old Pepe, the oldest child of a poor widow, is a lazy and stupid boy who spends most of his time practicing flicking the knife that is his only inheritance from his father, who had been killed by a rattlesnake. His mother is finally obliged to send him alone to Monterey for medicine. He tells her he is a man and can be trusted to go alone, but she calls him "a foolish chicken."[3] During a drunken quarrel in town, he kills a man who calls him names that—as a man—he cannot allow. He is obliged to flee into the mountains, where he is terrified by "a dark form against the sky, a man standing on top of a rock" (35). After his horse is shot from under him, he struggles, desperately thirsty, up the ragged slope, still hearing the faraway sounds of horses and dogs in pursuit. Exhausted, he falls asleep and loses track of his rifle. A cut that a stone has made between his fingers spreads infection to his whole arm.

As he struggles to the peak of the ridge, one bullet flies by him and a second hits him in the chest. He topples from the rock, starting a little avalanche that "slid down slowly and covered up his head" (46).

The brief story is like *Tortilla Flat* and *In Dubious Battle,* written during the same years of national depression and of despair in the author's life and based on the ancient rite of initiation into manhood, though in all three the individual is destroyed in the process because he is unprepared for the responsibilities demanded of an adult. Like other of Steinbeck's work, it is an essay of the loneliness of the individual who cannot or will not "split" as society demands. But no other of Steinbeck's works meets the stringent test of a "foredoomed loss of one reduced to the merest organism"; in the other *Long Valley* stories and other works, the author takes refuge in what Cady calls humanitarianism and Steinbeck's critics have branded sentimentalism. "Flight" provides a base point for understanding his capability for an objective presentation of the lone individual in an indifferent universe that permits a perception of his concept of culpability in cases of humans' inhumanity to other human beings, the behavior that links the other *Long Valley* stories as antipathetic to "Breakfast." Harry Teller's cry at the end of "The White Quail," "Oh, Lord, I'm so lonely" (*LV,* 42) might have come from characters in any of the group of stories.

"The White Quail"

Teller is lonely because his beautiful but neurotic wife has shut everyone else, including him, and everything but her garden out of her life. Early in the story, as Mary Teller looks at the dark hills beyond her perfect garden, she ponders, "That's the enemy. . . . That's the world that wants to get in, all rough and tangled and unkempt. But it can't get in because the fuchsias won't let it. That's what the fuchsias are for" (32). She chooses a husband after asking not "Would this man like such a garden?" but "Would the garden like such a man?" (30). Subsequently she locks him out of her bedroom. The climax in their relationship comes when she begins to identify with a rare albino quail in the garden and orders Harry to kill a cat that threatens it. He shoots the quail instead, then calls himself "a dirty skunk, to kill a thing she loves so much" (42). As a story of mismating (there are several in the group), this one is unquestionably presented from a masculine viewpoint yet the deeper issue it raises concerns the consequences of intimate relationships between human beings and external nature, an issue that caused problems for Steinbeck with a number of works, beginning with *To a God Unknown.*

"The Chrysanthemums"

Such a problem as utilized in "The Chrysanthemums" to deal with Elisa Allen and her prized flowers has intrigued more commentators to speculate on this story than on any other. Elisa has a green thumb, widely prized as indicating some kind of intimate relationship with external nature, but a limited knowledge of the manipulativeness of tradespeople (something Mary Teller questions as very devious). This limitation makes her vulnerable to exploitation by an itinerant tinker, who praises her beautiful flowers in order to get the pot from one of her plants. She sees the discarded plant on the road as her husband is driving her to town, and it makes her think briefly about having him take her to the prizefights to see the men hurt each other, though she finally rejects the idea.

Much of the critical discussion has focused on a single crucial word, after it was discovered that two slightly different versions of the story had been circulating unnoticed for some years. When the story was collected, it followed the original manuscript, which reads, following Elisa's catching sight of the discarded plant, "In a moment it was over. The thing was done. She did not look back" (22). In *Harper's* the first two sentences are replaced with this one: "In a moment they had left behind them the man who had not known or needed to know what she said, the bargainer."[3] The reasons for the difference are not known, but the editors may have made it—either to stress a point or to play down sexual innuendos that many commentators have observed in the story. Steinbeck revised the story for inclusion in *The Long Valley* but worked from the original manuscript and may not have consulted the *Harper's* text. In any event, the term *bargainer* does suggest some linkage of this story to his distaste for the tradesman's world that is often unaccountably neglected. All readers can know for sure, however, is that Elisa's relationship with her chrysanthemums is a lonely one.

"The Vigilante"

In "The Vigilante," which was originally titled "The Lonesome Vigilante," there is no doubt about the source of the title character's loneliness in sexual frustration. The story treats an actual lynching in Carol Steinbeck's home town of San Jose, but this shocking mob action provides in this story only the occasion for Steinbeck's revelation of a guy named Mike's participation in it, as he explains the reasons to a bartender: "There's times when citizens got to take the law into their own hands. Sneaky lawyer comes along and gets some fiend out of it" (*LV,* 90). But his underlying motivation is revealed when he gets home to his "thin, petulant wife" and is accused of having been with another woman. He denies the accusation but concludes she was right: "That's just exactly how I do feel" (95).

"The Murder"

Another disastrous marital situation is depicted in Steinbeck's first work to be selected for an annual national collection of prizewinning short stories. Again the husband literally gets away with murder in "The Murder." Jim Moore, a substantial Monterey county rancher, marries a Yugoslavian girl for her beauty, even though he is not "proud of her family" (*LV,* 173). Her father warns Moore that Slav girls are not like Americans and must be beaten, but Jim says he wouldn't do that. Jelka proves an admirable housekeeper and a passionate bedmate; however, Jim discovers "he could not get in touch with her in any way," and despite feeling "sorry for her loneliness," he spends his evenings having fun with some "noisy girls" in town, (174), while treating Jelka as a kind of prized possession.

One night he returns home early and finds her in bed with one of her male cousins, whom he shoots. The coroner assures him that charges of murder under such circumstances are always dismissed "in this part of the country." Jim goes home and beats Jelka, and then he tells her that he is going to build a new home and not whip her anymore—"for this" (186). Many readers are likely to find the story objectionable today, and one wonders what led the O. Henry Prize Committee in 1934 to prefer it over Steinbeck's others of the same period. As Patricia M. Mandia argues, however, while the characters in the story are racist and sexist, the author's ironic viewpoint is not. Again he is simply relating "something that happened" (the story even begins "This happened a number of years ago," suggesting that things may have since changed). But while Mandia's argument that "Steinbeck uses irony to point out that an American culture can be as violent, unjust, bigoted, and nonsensical as other cultures" is well supported,[5] Steinbeck's intentions are not as well realized in this story as in others in the collection, so that its singling out for recognition remains suspect.

"The Harness"

The full horror of the marital situation in the Randall household in "The Harness" has also not always been appreciated, because of Steinbeck's oversubtle conclusion. Peter Randall's sickly wife had forced him to wear a belt and harness to maintain his posture, but he had struck back by going once a year for a week's spree in San Francisco's "fancy houses," after which his wife Emma had a long annual bout of illness. After 21 years of this sadistic game-playing, "a long terrible illness" carries Emma off, and Peter breaks loose and gambles on a beautiful and fragrant but financially risky crop of sweet peas. His speculation pays off; he never repeats it, though, because even from beyond the grave she worried him about those sweet peas. This is not just a one-sided story about a sadomasochistic coupling that persisted even beyond the grave, however, because in the last sentences the burden of blame is shifted from Emma, who has seemed always to have held the upper hand, with Peter's almost throwaway revelation to a friend that next year, "I'm going to put in electric lights. Emma always wanted electric lights" (*LV*, 88).

One does not have to be married to suffer unpleasant experiences in life's long valley; three more stories broaden the author's montage without varying its predominating tones.

"The Snake"

"The Snake" relates, without authorial comment, an unexplained event that occurred in Ed Ricketts's laboratory when a tall woman appeared, bought a male rattlesnake, and then bought a rat and watched the snake eat it. The emphasis is placed, however, not on this grotesque proceeding but on the way it sickens the biologist as the woman begins to sway "just a suggestion," as the snake does before striking the rat. After the snake kills the rat and prepares to swallow it, "Dr. Phillips put his will against his head to keep from turning toward the woman. He thought, 'If she's opening her mouth, I'll be sick. I'll be afraid' " (*LV*, 56). He vows to leave her alone if she returns, but she never comes back.

"The Raid"

"The Raid" is a similarly objective account of another less bizarre but more common and appalling occasion for fear that foreshadows

Steinbeck's interest in labor disputes that will dominate his first successful conventional novel, *In Dubious Battle*. Two pathetically unprepared radical agitators are dreadfully beaten by vigilantes, but they survive the experience to meditate confusedly on their ordeal. The story differs from the others in the collection in that Root and Dick are sentimentalized in their devotion to a cause that is severely questioned in the novel to follow. The younger Root's vaguely religious stirrings also find less confused expression in Jim Casy's meditations in *The Grapes of Wrath*. The companionship of the two men also foreshadows *Of Mice and Men*. This inconclusive tale suggests something of the author's own uncertainties on his way to his major works.

"Johnny Bear"

While there seems no justification for placing these nine stories in any particular order stressing the developing of a theme, as in *The Pastures of Heaven*, the group would seem to come to a strongest climax by concluding with "Johnny Bear," the most intricately structured story, in which the titular character who seems the focus of attention proves to be only a device for penetrating a secret that must be kept from a whole community. The revelation of this secret about a respected citizen would have a devastating effect on communal morale. The story is also the only one besides "Breakfast," with its emphasis on a possible development of communal morale, to have a first-person narrator.

The story appears at first to be another example of Steinbeck's compassionate interest in subnormal characters. Like Tularecito in *The Pastures of Heaven* and Lennie in *Of Mice and Men,* Johnny Bear is described as a "half-wit," who can "photograph words and voices" and reproduce the conversation and intonations exactly, though he understands nothing of them. He is introduced here, however, only because his fondness for whiskey is gratified by repeating what he hears to the men at the local saloon, so that he becomes the vehicle through which a secret history becomes public.

The man who tells the narrator about Johnny also tells this outsider, "Every town has its aristocrats, its family above reproach. Emmalin and Amy Hawkins are our aristocrats. . . . They're symbols. They're what we tell our kids when we want to—well, to describe good people" (*LV,* 85). But the sisters are not exempt from Johnny Bear's eavesdropping. He reveals that the weaker of the two spinsters has become pregnant and hanged herself. Johnny's most staggering revelation, however, is that the father was Chinese—in the eyes of a small California town during the days of the Oriental Exclusion Act a member of a despised race. This woman, who in the eyes of the community has lived "as though honesty is the best policy and charity really is its own reward," suffered such loneliness that she had been driven to doubly proscribed behavior that could end only in suicide—one end of a long road.

Chapter Six
Dreams into Nightmares

The irony that modernist critics prized could scarcely be better illustrated than by Steinbeck's two grimmest pictures of dreams turning into nightmares, *In Dubious Battle* (1936) and *Of Mice and Men* (1937). These two works brought him the celebrity from which he would learn sadly that fame ruins everyone, just as he had thought.

In Dubious Battle

Steinbeck's first successful conventionally organized novel has begun to suffer as time has passed from what had earlier often been praised as its principal merit of being the best strike novel written during the decade of great labor unrest—the depression years of the 1930s. Because of Steinbeck's desire to treat objectively an inflammatory partisan subject and because it was based on information gathered from radical organizers working in the fields with the migrant pickers on California farms, it is often treated as a fictional document, leading to judgments like Harold Bloom's that it is "now quite certainly a period piece. . . . of more interest to social historians than to literary critics" (Bloom, 1). Those treating the work as a textbook—and surely such a book would not have survived the vicissitudes of readers' tastes for more than half a century—will be misled. Despite's Steinbeck's assertions, on the one hand, that he had used accurate information from reliable sources and, on the other, as he wrote a friend, "I'm not interested in strikes, as a means of raising men's wages, and I'm not interested in ranting about justice and oppression, mere outcroppings which indicate the condition" (*Life*, 98), he had made no effort to produce the record of any particular strike or any typical strike of the period (if there is such a thing). Rather the strike depicted here serves only as the backdrop for the tragedy of an individual—a unique human being—engaged in "dubious battle."

Problems of the intentions behind the novel are complicated by the ambiguity of the word *dubious*, borrowed from Milton's description of Lucifer's uprising against God in *Paradise Lost*—though it could scarcely be claimed that the "battle" in Steinbeck's novel had such cosmic dimensions. What they share is ironically that, on a literal level, the outcome of neither is ever in doubt. Just as Lucifer was foredoomed not to triumph over God's omnipotence, the odds in Steinbeck's earthly confrontation are hopelessly against the nervous strikers from the beginning, as the strike organizers realize when they learn how thoroughly the growers have prepred for concerted action. What is dubious about this battle is not its outcome but its causes and its consequences. Why should factions be driven to such violence against each other, and who finally are the losers in such a struggle despite temporary victories? What was the "condition" that concerned Steinbeck that these "outcroppings" merely indicated? He wrote to a friend who he was glad had liked the novel, "I still think that most 'realistic' writing is farther from the real than the most honest fantasy. The Battle with its tricks to make a semblance of reality wasn't very close" (Benson, 325). Understanding the novel depends, on perceiving the significance of his "honest fantasy."

Part of this fantasy was that, though Steinbeck insisted that all of the incidents he depicted were based on actual events his informants had related to him, they were drawn from different times and different strikes in different regions and that he had changed even the geography of California to keep his narrative from being associated with any particular strike and to avoid the exposure of his sources. A more important part was that his central figure did not have any real-life counterpart but was invented—in part from his own experiences not as a labor organizer but as an aspiring writer trying to fulfill his ambitions and find his own place in society—to embody his conception of the individual's "condition" in the contemporary world.

It must be recalled that Steinbeck wrote this novel before receiving any substantial recognition from the publication of *Tortilla Flat*. During this period he was still despairing about his own prospects and was writing—not imitatively or merely fashionably like the "proletarian" writers of the time, with whom he was frequently confused during the late 1930s,[1] but to share the ironic modernist vision manifested in all his novels, from *Cup of Gold* to *Of Mice and Men*. A much more alienated and despairing man than wrote *The Grapes of Wrath* staked his hopes on *In Dubious Battle*.

Involving a character with his own temperament in events in which Steinbeck had no participatory experience turns this narrative into something more than a historic document—it becomes an archetypal account of one young man's battle to make a place for himself in an uncaring, manipulative society—an effort that offers always dubious prospects and on this occasion ends in disaster.

From the curt opening sentence, "At last it was evening," to the unfinished final line, "he didn't want a thing for himself—," the focus of the narrative is narrowly on Jim Nolan as he moves from the oncoming darkness in the city in the twilight[2] to a faceless darkness in the bloody fields. Jim is scarcely ever out of the reader's sight during the last nine days of his life, as he moves inexorably from the only lighted office in a decaying building where he is recruited for "the party" to the "almost complete darkness of the woods" where he dies for it. At the center of every scene, no matter who the principal players, is what Jim does and, more important, what he sees and learns. Instead of a panoramic view of a strike Steinbeck offers an impressionistic view of how one young man, newly initiated into such a scene, perceives and participates in it. Even the much-praised objectivity of the book is in one respect illusory, for while the author avoids taking sides, we follow the action through the spotlighting of a figure that has. (A reason that the account is somewhat unbalanced by its not presenting scenes of the growers' councils is that Jim would not be privy to them, though he listens to their spokesman.)

In Dubious Battle is thus not an anatomy of a 1930s strike, which would soon be dated social history, but a bildungsroman, a term we borrow from the German because no word in English encompasses its complex meaning of presenting any process of growth from immaturity to maturity, physical, mental, or spiritual.

While this process of maturing usually takes years, Jim is on a crash course. When we meet him in his lonely, twilight room, he is confused and despondent, without any sense of purpose; eight days later he has discovered a latent cunning and developed the confidence to take command of a deteriorating situation from older and more experienced hands. He has made remarkable progress, proving himself an apt and resourceful student who quickly develops leadership abilities. Steinbeck as aspiring author is not, however, as much concerned with Jim's contribution to the particular cause that has recruited him as he is with the revelation that a gifted and quick-witted young person is *not* appreciated by an apathetic society suspicious and resentful of talent and *is* exploited by fanatics devoted to a cause that they have not examined carefully. The objectivity of the novel lies in Steinbeck's balancing portrayals of what, after a post–World War II tour of the Soviet Union, he would describe in 1948 as "the ecclesiastical Left and the lumpen Right," both of which are presented with passionate subjectivity from the viewpoint of a gifted and aggressive young critic.

Twelve years earlier Steinbeck had demonstrated what he meant when he wrote to his friend Louis Paul, "I don't like communists either. I mean I dislike them as people. I rather imagine the apostles had the same waspish qualities and the New Testament is proof that they had equally bad manners" (*Life*, 120). Steinbeck was not a revolutionist (he becomes almost hysterical at times in *The Grapes of Wrath* in trying to warn readers to act to avert revolution); he was like many genuinely well-intentioned people who wanted to improve society to their own advantage without hurting others. In a short time he was to enjoy extraordinary success; then, like many others, he did not know what do do with it.

Steinbeck's subsequent life had some nightmarish aspects, but he survived to reap deserved honors. He did not experience the fate he foresaw for Jim Nolan. Jim was a victim, however, as Steinbeck viewed the world he shared with the character, of neither the contending party that exploited him nor the one that curtly rejected him, but rather an entire society that had wandered into a dehumanized wasteland by insisting on mindless conformity. Steinbeck at this point refused to take sides in provincial conflicts, but he was passionately partisan in individuals' struggles for self-determination.

Of Mice and Men

Although there is no evidence that Steinbeck had any conscious intention of shaping the three novels concluding with *Of Mice and Men* into a kind of ironic trilogy about man's fate, viewed jointly as a phase in an artist's development, they do provide a vision of the three principal forces that are responsible for the "going under" of one who refuses, in the words of Sir Henry Morgan, to "split" before "civilization." Danny in *Tortilla Flat* finds it impossible to accept the responsibilties of living in respectable society but also finds it impossible to return to a wild life of natural freedom, and so he destroys himself. Jim Nolan in *In Dubious Battle* is destroyed by the enemy because he has developed a sense of mission too quickly to carry it out with enough caution. George in *Of Mice and Men* is forced to destroy his own dream because, like the grandfather's in *The Red Pony,* its fulfillment is impossible because of irredeemable shortcomings of nature.

Originally Steinbeck had in mind a work for children, to be called "Something That Happened" and to emphasize from a nonteleological viewpoint the absence of any external controlling force responsible for causing the events depicted. The series of events takes place over one weekend after two migrant farmhands arrive at a new employer's ranch after having had to run away from an earlier job because Lennie, one of them, has great strength but a fondness for soft objects like mice and rabbits and is unable to control his actions. George has known him from childhood and feels responsible for him, since Lennie has no kin. They share a dream of owning a little ranch of their own where they can raise rabbits. The dream is shattered, however, when Lennie unwittingly kills first a mouse and then a puppy and finally the young wife of the ranch owner's son when the lonely woman insists he feel her soft hair. Lennie has already broken the husband Curley's hand when he had insisted on fighting the powerful but reluctant hired man, and Curley sets off with a posse to lynch Lennie. George steals a Luger (a pistol used by the German Nazis) from another farmhand, who displays no human feeling and, having told Lennie where to hide in the event of trouble, goes there and kills him himself before the enraged crowd can find him, as they recite for the last time their ritualized dream of their farm.

The pessimistic vision behind the tale is articulated by a crippled stablebuck, Crooks—one of the few important black characters in Steinbeck's fiction—who lives in lonely isolation, ostracized from the communal bunkhouse. In an attack on the proletarian novelists' vision of a worker's paradise, Crooks explains, "I seen hunderds of men come by on the road an' on the ranches, with their bindles on their back an' that same damn thing in their heads. . . . [E]very damn one of 'ems got a little piece of land in his head. An' never a God damn one of 'em ever gets it. Just like heaven. . . . Nobody ever gets to heaven, and nobody gets no land."[3]

Critics have made efforts to argue that the ending of the novel, when Slim, the wise foreman at the ranch, takes George up the trail for a drink, offers a ray of hope that makes this story less defeatist than *Tortilla Flat* and *In Dubious Battle*. Steinbeck gives the last word not to Slim, however, but to the insensitive owner of the Luger—with all its fascist symbolism—who says to the sadistic Curley, "Now what the hell ya suppose is eatin' them two guys?" Steinbeck is still presenting an unfeeling world where any sign of human caring is exploited as a weakness. Slim can understand situations and momentarily ameliorate them, but he cannot cure them. George has been forced to destroy by his own hand a dream that cannot be revived.

Few comments by Steinbeck while writing this work have been published, but a remarkable letter that he wrote to actress Claire Luce while she was playing Curley's wife on Broadway shows much about his detailed conception of characters that can only be hinted at in published texts, as well as about the misanthropic mood he was in while composing this work. A member of his agents' staff had written him that the actress was beginning to have misgivings about her interpretation of the part. Steinbeck pointed out that "she was trained by threat not only at home but by other kids. . . . She learned she had to be hard to cover her fright. . . . She is a nice, kind girl and not a floozy. No man has ever considered her as anything except a girl to make. . . . She is afraid of everyone in the world. . . . [Girls like that] pretend to be wise and hard and voluptuous" (*Life*, 155).

While he was writing this novel, Steinbeck had just been through problems over the acceptance of *In Dubious Battle,* he was uncomfortable and frightened himself by celebrity, a puppy had destroyed about two months' work on the book, he was depressed as his success made old friends envious, and he had to project a tough image to protect himself from importunings. His letter to Claire Luce suggests that he was again projecting many of his own problems through his characters'. The world as he saw it at this point was dominated by the unfeeling Curleys and Carlsons, and there was no resting place before the grave for innocents like Curley's wife or George and Lennie.

Perhaps this is a young person's book after all—not for small children but for teenagers (and it has become one of the most widely used modern novels in high schools)—precisely because of its disillusioning message that dreams can be dangerous and destructive. Steinbeck's own next effort was to try to write a book in which from his own report he tried to be wise and hard, but he could not go through with its publication. Instead he wrote *The Grapes of Wrath.*

Chapter Seven

The Education of the Heart

The Grapes of Wrath

In the interval between the theatrical production of *Of Mice and Men* and the publication of the *The Grapes of Wrath*, Steinbeck's vision underwent a drastic change from the bleak modernism of the two previous novels and most of his short stories. The gap was longer than appears from his publication record, because most of the stories in *The Long Valley* had been written before he turned from his novelette/play to the "big" novel he had been planning for some time, growing out of his observation of the plight of the Dust Bowl migrants in California.

Although we cannot isolate just what triggered this turnabout from desperate defeatism to militant idealism, it appears to have occurred quite suddenly in 1938, after his traumatic visits to flooded areas where migrant workers had been trapped. As he became increasingly dissatisfied with what he had been writing, he finally destroyed a complete manuscript he was preparing to send to Covici and began a work entirely different from anything that had preceded it.

We have no idea of the tone and viewpoint of the first of four starts to treat this material in a work tentatively titled "The Oklahomans," a study of the conditions of the migrants' lives. Robert DeMott, who has made the most exhaustive study of this period in connection with his editing of *Working Days*—a journal that Steinbeck kept day by day while writing what was to become *The Grapes of Wrath*—thinks he had done little actual writing, indicative of his uncertainty about how to best treat fictionally the problems he had reported factually for a newspaper, (*Working Days*, xxxvi). We know from his apologetic letter to his agents that he destroyed the pretentiously titled "L'Affaire Lettuceberg" after completing it, because it was a "smart alec" attack on the controlling cabal of businessmen in his hometown of Salinas. Some hint of what the story was like may be provided by a short story that he later published obscurely after deleting it from *Cannery Row*, because of its treatment of Salinas. On other occasions he had spared from the destruction of outgrown works some particularly favorite pieces, such as "Saint Katy the Virgin."

"The Time the Wolves Ate the Vice-Principal" is a bitterly cynical attack on a smug community's lack of awareness of dangers that immediately confront it. In its macabre conclusion a pack of hungry wolves kill the overworked vice-principal of the city high school as he attempts to get home on foot while the complacent bourgeoisie sleeps. Previously it was supposed that the story was cut from *Cannery Row* because of the publishers' objections to the distasteful subject matter; however, Roy Simmonds's studies of the manuscript have established that it had been cut before the manuscript was completed, not, he theorizes, because of the subject matter but because it took place inland in Salinas, not in Monterey, the setting for the novel. If this story was not in keeping with the bittersweet wistfulness of Steinbeck's tale of the littoral, it would certainly fit into what we know of "L'Affaire Lettuceberg." If so, the text that Steinbeck destroyed must have been a shockingly unpleasant one indeed, venting his disgust about the irresponsibility of the community's respectable citizens.

This possibility is particularly intriguing, because if *The Grapes of Wrath* ended with the death of ex-preacher Jim Casy, the structure of its narrative—excluding the interchapters—would closely resemble those of *In Dubious Battle, Of Mice and Men,* and the puzzling short story as another record of an apocalyptic view of a world without hope.

The Grapes of Wrath is not, however, limited to the tragic story of the vicious slaughter of a person who has undergone a spiritual transformation. Casy serves only as the vehicle for the transformation of Tom Joad from a selfish, violent individual concerned only with the survival of his touchy clan into a visionary operating selflessly in the background as an inspiring influence to his whole community.

It is Casy's doctrine that "There ain't no sin and there ain't no virtue. There's just stuff people do. . . . Maybe all men got one big soul everybody's a part of."[1] The relationship of this vision of things to Ralph Waldo Emerson's transcendentalist concept of the oversoul has been remarked by many critics since Frederic Carpenter's trailblazing essay, "The Philosophical Joads" in 1941.[2] Although Steinbeck shrugged off any transcendentalist affiliations, there is a reference in *The Sea of Cortez* to any investigation carried far enough bringing to light psychic or spiritual "residua, or rather [leaving] them still unassailable as Emerson remarked a hundred years ago in 'The Oversoul,' "[3] but Steinbeck turns to Emerson—as the essayist would have approved—for support rather than as a source for a line of thinking he had developed in conjunction with his conversations with Ed Ricketts. Certainly Steinbeck cannot be pigeonholed as a consistent disciple of transcendentalism, even if such discipleship would not violate Emerson's rejection of conformity and consistency and Steinbeck's refusal to follow before World War II any party line. Casy is not, like Jim Nolan in *In Dubious Battle,* a martyr to a particular ideology but one of those who would rather "go under" with honor than "split" before a corrupt civilization. Unlike Joseph Wayne in *To a God Unknown,* however, he does have a message that wins converts, so that, as his initials unsubtly signify, he becomes "a new Christ here in the West."

The Grapes of Wrath ends with what remains of the Joad family seeking refuge from the floods in a barn where Rose of Sharon, abandoned by her husband, who has split in several senses, at the urgings of technological civilization, offers the milk of her breast, intended for her stillborn baby, to a dying old man—an incredibly beautiful tableau that *New Yorker* reviewer Clifton Fadiman found "the tawdriest kind of fake symbolism."[4] They are far from achieving their goal or even ensuring their survival. What will happen is left to the "Dear Reader" whom Charles Dickens addresses at the end of *Hard Times* (a title Steinbeck might certainly also have used): "It rests with you and me, whether in our two fields of action, similar things shall be or not. Let them be!"

The story of the Joads, thus, insofar as it concerns the novelist in his field of action, is completed in the barn. The solution of the social problems underlying the fictional action is something Steinbeck, like Dickens, leaves to the daily business of the readers. While Steinbeck has abandoned the dogmatic pessimism of his earlier fiction, he certainly provides no happy ending. The novel is not about the family's finding security; it is about their education, the completion of which is shown in the final scene.

What "education"? The education of the heart, the same kind that Thomas Gradgrind received painfully in *Hard Times,* after having been responsible, as Dickens shows, for the miseducation of a younger generation. In *The Grapes of Wrath* this education results in a change from the family's proudly isolating itself as part of a self-important clan to its accepting a role as part of one vast human family that, in Casy's words, shares "one big soul ever-body's a part of." The novel is less concerned with the frustrations of enforced physical migration than with an accompanying spiritual movement akin to the one celebrated in Walt

Whitman's "Passage to India": "back to wisdom's birth, to innocent
intuitions."

Casy has already meditated on the idea of one human family before he
meets the Joads, but he cannot clearly formulate his concept that
"maybe it's all men an' all women we love" (32), because "fella gets use'
to a way of thinkin', it's hard to leave" (69). When he finds confirmation
of his theory in the observation of Muley Graves, who will not leave his
land, that "If a fella's got somepin to eat an' another fella's hungry—
why the first fella ain' got no choice," Casy feels obliged to say, "Muley's
got a-holt of sompin, an' it's too big for him, an it's too big for me" (66).
He is able to articulate his new vision, however, when he replies to Ma
Joad's dogma that cutting pork is women's work, "It's all work. . . .
They's too much of it to split up to men's or women's work" (146).

When Casy finally figures out in a California jail what he does believe,
he explains his ideas in the form of a parable that illustrates the benefits
of unified action. Describing the inmates as "nice fellas" who turned bad
because "they needed stuff," he explains what happened one day when
they were served sour beans: "One fella started yellin', an nothin' happened. . . . Then another fella yelled. Well, sir, then we all got yellin'.
And we all got on the same tone. . . . Then somepin happened. They
come a-runnin', and they give us some other stuff to eat—give it to us.
Ya see?" (521–22). At the moment Tom Joad does not; Casy observes,
"Maybe I can't tell you. . . . Maybe you got to find out" (522). The novel
depicts the Joads' "finding out."

They are a difficult case, for the Joads are *not* "such *good* poor people"
as Lionel Trilling condescendingly called them in a review that articu-
lates the hostility of the New York intelligentsia to the novel and its
author.[5] The novel does not "cocker-up the self-righteousness of the liberal middle class" with a fantasy of the conversion of the easily suscepti-
ble. They are proud and violent people, with "a low threshold of insult,"
like these who Steinbeck himself would say only a few years later, in *The
Wayward Bus,* disappear "from the face of the earth." Their haughty, isolated attitude at the beginning of the novel is illustrated by Tom's
remark to a friendly but nosy truck driver: "Nothin' ain't none of your
affair except skinnin' this here bull-bitch along, an' that's the least thing
you work at" (18). Tom is no thinker. When Casy tells him, "They's
gonna come a thing that's gonna change the whole country," Tom
replies, "I'm stil layin' my dogs down one at a time" (237).

Ma, whom Steinbeck calls "the citadel of the family" (100), views the
migration to California only in terms of the family's getting a little white

house and burns a few pathetic souvenirs of the past matter-of-fatly. When Tom asks her if she's not scared that the new place won't be as nice as they hope, she replies, "No, I ain't. . . . Up ahead they's a thousan' lives we might live, but when it comes, it'll on'y be one . . . it's jus' the road goin' by for me. . . . All the rest'd get upset if I done any more'n that" (168–69). When she threatens Pa with a jack-handle to prevent the family's splitting up, she argues, "All we got is the family unbroke. Like a bunch of cows when the lobos are ranging, stick all together. I ain't scared while we're all here, all that's alive, but I ain't gonna see us bust up" (231). She seeks rationalizations that will incorporate the Wilsons, who help them, into the family, rather than acknowledge the kindness of strangers: "We got almost a kin bond. Grampa, he died in your tent." She will not let Casy write the note to be pinned to Grampa's body, because he "wan't no kin" (195).

Despite her brave efforts and bold protests, the family disintegrates. First the dog is killed on the highway. Then Grampa dies of a stroke before the family leaves Oklahoma. Granma dies before they reach the fertile valleys of California. Because each death represents an inability to adjust to a changing lifestyle, Ma is most shaken by the departure of one of the younger generation, oldest son Noah, to live "beside a nice river," and she ruefully observes, "Family's fallin' apart. . . . I don' know. Seems like I can't think no more" (294). Most alarming is the sneaky departure of Rose of Sharon's husband, as his running away shatters a potential family unit while she is pregnant with their first child.

Ma's pride suffers other blows. She first hears the disparaging term *Okie* when a California border patrolman tells her, "We don't want none of you settlin' down here" (291). Then she is upset by the vigilance committee, which warns the family, "We ain't gonna have no goddam Okies in this town" (382). Still, she thinks only in terms of the clan. Her reaction upon arriving in Bakersfield is "the fambly's here" (311), and during the encounter with the vigilantes she counsels Tom to do nothing because "the fambly's breakin' up" (381).

The first significant change in the Joads' attitude occurs in the Weedpatch government camp, where a family named Wallace share their work with Tom, although they may thereby cut their own meager earnings. The self-governing arrangement at this camp also makes the Joads feel like decent people again. Evaluating her recent experiences, Ma says, "in Needles, that police. He done somepin to me, made me feel mean. Made me feel ashamed. An' now I ain't ashamed. . . . I feel like people again" (420). But she prefaces her remarks with the reminder

"We're Joads." Nor is all harmonious at the camp: a religious bigot attacks Rose of Sharon, and the women stage a garbage fight. Pa is far from Casy's way of thinking—"I can't starve so's you can get two bits," he tells another man during a quarrel about taking strikers' jobs for lower wages (463).

The easy atmosphere of the government camp, where one man observes, "We're all a-workin' together" (488), is in chilling contrast to the tense atmosphere at the Hooper Ranch, where the prevailing paranoia is epitomized by a checker's explanation that putting holes in the bottom of buckets "keeps people from stealing them" (506). Here Ma learns "one thing good": "If you're in trouble or hurt or need—go to poor people. They're the only ones that'll help—the only ones" (513–14). The Joads, however, still think of help as only a means toward maintaining their family. When Casy, now a labor organizer, pleads with Tom to support a strike against the ranch, Tom replies, "Pa wouldn't do it. . . . He'd say it wasn't none of his business. . . . Think Pa's gonna give up his meat on account a other fellas?" (524).

A family crisis is precipitated at this ranch by Tom's impetuously killing the man who kills Casy. Tom decides he must run away, but Ma retorts angrily that "goin' away ain't gonna ease us. It's gonna bear us down. . . . We was always one thing—we was the fambly—kinda whole and clear. An' now we ain't clear no more. . . . There ain't no fambly now" (536). Her suspicion of any idea beyond family loyalty appears in telling Tom he can't go, "They wouldn' be no way to hide out. You couldn' trus' nobody. But you can trus' us. We can hide you" (545–46).

Although they leave that ranch, a major change has occurred by the time Tom and Ma have a final conversation. Young Ruthie has undone the family by boasting about Tom's outlaw exploits. Ma realizes then that Tom must leave. While hiding, he has been thinking over Casy's ideas, and when Ma tells him she is worried that she may not know what becomes of him, he tells her, in a speech that became famous after Henry Fonda delivered it in John Ford's film version of the novel, "Well, maybe like Casy says, a fella ain't got a soul of his own, but on'y a piece of a big one. . . . Then it don' matter. Then I'll be all aroun' in the dark. I'll be ever'where—wherever you look. Wherever there's a fight so hungry people can eat. . . . An' when our folks eat the stuff they raise an' live in the houses they build—why I'll be there" (572). The concept of clan loyalty has been replaced by the idea that one must help whoever needs help.

Pa learns this lesson of cooperation during the building of a dam to hold floodwaters out of a cotton-pickers' camp, and he cries, "We can do her if ever'body helps" (595). Most important, Ma's acceptance of the idea of a responsibility beyond the family is shown after her last meeting with Tom, in her conversation with a neighbor whom she thanks for helping during Rose of Sharon's labor:

> The stout woman smiled, "No need to thank.
> Ever'body's in the same wagon. S'pose we was down.
> You'd give us a han'."
> "Yes," Ma said, "we would."
> "Or anybody."
> "Or anybody. Use' ta be the fambly was fust. It ain't so now. It's anybody. Worse off we get, the more we got to do." (606)

But while this dialogue accepts the spirit of Casy's idea of universal brotherhood, it does not translate its meaning into action. Some concluding gesture must indicate that the education of the heart has transformed behavior.

The opportunity arises in the barn where the refugees from the flood discover the famished man. Ma's unstated suggestion that Rose of Sharon give him her milk carries into practice the idea that "worse off we get, the more we got to do." Having come to the barn with almost nothing, the family, through Rose of Sharon, gives the one thing it has left—the most intimate gift it could offer. This tableau in the barn does not break off an unfinished story; it marks the end of the story that Steinbeck had to tell about the Joads. They have completed their education by transcending familial prejudices. What happens now to them—to anyone—depends on the ability of the rest of society to learn what the Joads have learned. The point of this story is neither obscure nor tragic. *The Grapes of Wrath* is an epic comedy of the triumph of the holy spirit.

Structure and Meaning

Readers may, however, become so involved in the fortunes of particular characters that the universal implications of a novel or other literary work may be overlooked. Trying to avoid the problem that *The Grapes of Wrath* would be interpreted as the unique account of one family's troubled pilgrimage, Steinbeck paired the chapters narrating the history of the Joads with others that show the broader significance of the things that happen to them.

Although nowhere in the novel (or in his later published journal of its writing) does the author identify the method he is using, he does carefully explain—as Peter Lisca pointed out in *The Wide World of John Steinbeck*[6]—a conscious intention behind his procedure in his preface to the voice-over narrative from his film *The Forgotten Village* (1941), illustrated with stills from the film. Commenting on the problems he faced in creating this account of the introduction of scientific medicine into a remote, superstition-ridden Mexican village, Steinbeck explained, "A great many documentary films have used the generalized method, that is, the showing of a condition or an event as it affects a group of people. . . . In *The Forgotten Village* we reversed the usual process. Our story centered on one family in one small village. We wished our audience to know this family very well, and incidentally to like it, as we did. Then, from association with this little personalized group, the larger conclusion concerning the racial group can be drawn with something like participation."[7] In *The Grapes of Wrath* Steinbeck had not taken a chance on one method or the other; he had used both to help get his points across. The Joad story, like *The Forgotten Village,* focuses on one family, while the "generalized method" is used in the interchapters. By presenting the situations that distressed him through the history of one family, he obliged readers to visualize the affected individuals and denied escapists the distancing consolation of the sociology textbooks' treatment of problem groups in numbers too large to be easily comprehended.

On the other hand, by using the generalized method he refuted any charges that the history of the Joads was unique and solely fictional. In the device of the interchapter he found exactly the technique he needed to make his "big" novel simultaneously a general tract and an intensely personal history of the frightening situation of a culture in transition.

This last description, however, limits the novel too much to a depiction of a particular time and place. The novel is more than a period piece about a troubled past era; it is also an allegory, applicable wherever prejudice and a haughty sense of self-importance inhibit cooperation.

In a letter to Pascal Covici in January 1939, defending the final scene of the novel and refusing to change it, Steinbeck stressed that there are "five layers in this book," "a reader will find as many as he can," and "what he takes from it will be scaled entirely on his own depth or hollowness" (*Life,* 178). Nothing so far published provides any specific indication of his conception of these five layers, but speculation might well begin with the most famous explanation of "levels of meaning" in literature, which comes from St. Thomas Aquinas but is most usefully presented by Dante, who drew on Aquinas in *Convivio:*

> Exposition must be *literal* and *allegorical*. And for the understanding of this you should know that writings can be understood and must be explained, for the most part, in four senses. One is called *literal;* and this is the one which extends not beyond the letter itself. The next is called *allegorical;* and this is the one which is hidden beneath the cloak of these fables. . . . The third sense is called *moral;* and this is the one which readers must ever diligently observe in writings, for their own profit and for that of their pupils. . . . The fourth sense is called *anagogical* or or supersensual; and this is when we expound spiritually a writing which, even in the letter, through the very things exprest expresseth things concerning eternal glory.[8]

In a famous letter to his friend Can Grande della Scala, Dante, explaining his own *Divine Comedy,* applied these concepts to the biblical story of the Exodus from Egypt, which many critics argue influenced *The Grapes of Wrath*: "If we look to the *letter* alone, we are told of the going forth of the children from Egypt in the time of Moses; if we look at the *allegory,* we are told of our future redemption through Christ; if we consider the *moral* sense, we are told of the conversion of the soul from the grief and misery of sin to the state of grace; if we consider the *anagogical,* we are told of the going forth of the blessed soul from the servitude of corruption to the freedom of eternal glory.[9]

Literal and allegorical levels of *The Grapes of Wrath* have already been examined in this chapter as the history of the Joads' migration and the illustration of an education of the heart. On the moral level it has already been suggested that Steinbeck, like Dickens, is expressing outrage that such conditions exist and pleading for readers to play their part in alleviating and eliminating them. On the anagogical level Tom Joad may achieve a sense of "eternal glory" when he speaks lyrically of being "all aroun' in the dark," though this might seem still too earthbound for a saintly vision.

Steinbeck speaks of a fifth layer. May individuality be transcended altogether through the "one big soul" Casy speaks about? What does Steinbeck mean in chapter 14 by "Manself" that has the one quality distinctive in the universe of suffering and dying for a concept? Is Steinbeck suggesting a layer of experience at which individual distinctions are obliterated in something like Emerson's "oversoul"?

Whatever he may have had in mind, *The Grapes of Wrath*, when contemplated in this questioning manner, can be seen as not just the story of Okies' migration, of the perpetual pursuit of an Arcadian dream, of human injustices and their potential rectification through enlightenment, or even the final reward promised the pure in heart, but also as the unique and endless story of the strivings of a life force transcending individuals to endure and triumph over obstacles that beset its way—something that Steinbeck was not to aspire toward in his subsequent work.

Chapter Eight
Wartime Search for a Hero

After publishing *The Grapes of Wrath* in 1939, Steinbeck faced the unexpectedly formidable problem of what to do next. A publisher's dream is to develop a novelist like J. P. Marquand, who, after a promising apprenticeship, turns out a novel that is a popular and critical success like *The Late George Apley* (1937) and then turns out a succession of books about a diversity of characters and situations that satisfy audience expectations by following the same general pattern, as Marquand did from 1941 to 1955, while phasing out his earlier potboilers (like the Mr. Moto series of detective stories). Steinbeck was under pressure for the first time to follow again the pattern of his novel about a great national sociopolitical problem, although his own tendency had always been not to repeat himself but to experiment constantly with something new. He was also exhausted by the drive to produce by far the longest work he had written and was disoriented just as much by the enthusiastic reception it received in some quarters as by the virulent attack on the novel and himself from others. For a time he even considered giving up fiction altogether and turning to scientific writing, such as "The Log" from *Sea of Cortez*. Complications in his private life and the onset of World War II also made unprecedented demands on him.

Steinbeck's choices were further complicated because even had he wished to continue to examine the crisis posed in his home state by the migrant workers, the immediate problem had been unexpectedly solved in the most abhorrent manner. The nation's increasing involvement in the war led to the quick absorption of the excess population by booming defence industries and increased agricultural production even before the official investigation of the treatment of the migrants was completed.

Steinbeck, however, had never been principally interested in the sociopolitical and economic aspects of the situations he had dealt with fictionally. Both *In Dubious Battle* and *The Grapes of Wrath*, which publishers and public had hoped would provide the model for his future work, are not so much about the strikes depicted and the conditions fomenting them as about the emergence and fate of those who might prove to be inspired leaders of the people. Steinbeck was still basically interested in heroes, as he had been as a young writer. In this one aspect he had begun to repeat himself in portrayals from *Cup of Gold* to *Of Mice and Men* of a sequence of idealistic dreamers whose dreams are doomed by insensitive materialists. He had finally produced in Tom Joad, working with what many critics found "raw" material indeed, a heroic figure who continued to inspire the efforts of his people, though from a distance and with no assurance of success.

In doing so, however, he had written himself up a blind alley, for not only would he have been impatient with repetitions but also the urgent situation of a world at war demanded the inspiring example of more active freedom fighters. Steinbeck was not to return to the half-mythical hero until he did begin to repeat himself a decade hence, in his apotheosis of the Mexican leader Emiliano Zapata for a film that is one of his best works of the period but was not widely circulated because of the producers' fear as political reprisals.

In the meantime he faced the problem of a viable hero—one who set a practical example without becoming corrupted, who refuted Henry Morgan's cynical apothegm by neither splitting nor going under.

For a start he turned to a new setting, Mexico—which had always intrigued him—and a new medium, film, and returned to the model of *The Red Pony* to produce his first genuinely optimistic work, dealing with a youth who might become both a practical and an idealistic leader of the people—as Jody Tiflin had only wished he might be. Although it is beautifully executed, there is for the first time in this work that has never become widely known because of the difficulty of access to it an element of ambiguity in the author's relationship to the audience, because though it impresses one as a documentary, an actual case study, it is an entirely fictional work using an actual geographic setting and native, nonprofessional actors.

The Forgotten Village

The story line of *The Forgotten Village* (1941), delivered through voice-over narrative problem of the difficulty of bringing expensive sound equipment to the location, where the dialogue in an Indian tongue would have had to be subtitled anyway, is extremely simple. A village is threatened by an epidemic that is not yielding to the traditional remedies of the *curandera* (wise woman), an indigenous witch doctor. The local schoolteacher tries to induce the villagers to understand the bacterial cause of the epidemic—the polluted water of the village well—and to call in scientifically trained doctors from Mexico City, but he meets with bitter resistance from the superstitious natives. One of his pupils, however, Juan Diego, who has lost a younger brother to the epidemic, trusts the teacher and breaks with his family to make a perilous journey alone to the city and bring back a medical team that detoxifies the well. Then he decides that he will return to the city to be trained as a doctor who will bring the benefits of modern medicine back to his people. The significance of the boy's work is pointed out by a soldier whom he meets on the way to the city: "Yours is the true people's work . . . saving, not killing; growing, not dying." Although the narrator universalizes the subject by assuring viewers that "there are thousands of Juan Diegos in the villages of Mexico," the film ends with a close-up of the boy's face as he proclaims, "I am Juan Diego," stressing the dedication of an inspired individual to become a leader of the people.

The difference between the conclusion of this slight work and that of the massive *Grapes of Wrath* is that the heroic survivor is no longer a shadowy figure inspiring his people from a distance; he is an active campaigner who will work among the crowd like Jim Nolan, not as a leader or in dubious battle but as a guide to precautionary measures that will ensure healthy lives. Steinbeck's friend Ed Ricketts had misgivings about this script that led to one of the most serious misunderstandings between them, because Ricketts observed in an "anti-script" that Juan Diego becomes "so imbued with the spirit of modern medical progress that he leaves the traditional way of his people to associate himself with the new thing" (Astro, *JS&R*, 59). Ricketts's concerns remain a serious issue, as misgivings persist, for example, about the World Health Organization's success in eradicating fatal childhood diseases if economic opportunities are not improved along with physical cures to prevent a thriving population's facing threats of starvation. Steinbeck was trying with naive enthusiasm to recommend the imposition on a still primitive society of a life-style for which it was not adequately prepared, as he would also in *The Pearl*.

An example of Steinbeck's moving too fast for the times, even in his supposedly sophisticated homeland, was provided by a battle with New York censors over scenes of childbirth in *The Forgotten Village*. By the time this problem was resolved, with Eleanor Roosevelt's intervention, the United States's entry into World War II resulted in the film's attracting almost no notice when it was finally released.

The Moon Is Down

The maturity of the American public was also brought seriously into question by a curiously divided response to Steinbeck's second novelette/play, which was his first direct response to World War II, begun before the Pearl Harbor attack. While *The Moon Is Down* (1942) was coolly and even angrily received both as fiction and as drama in the United States, it proved to be one of his most successful and admired works in occupied Europe. The emotional reasons for this dichotomy are largely unrelated to its artistic merits; hence it has become difficult to view the work objectively, although—possibly more than any other work of Steinbeck's—it is neither so good nor so bad as generally supposed.

The problems in the United States began with the final work's not being the one Steinbeck wanted to write. He originally proposed to depict the invasion of an American community, resembling Monterey, California, by an invading foreign army, but this idea was vetoed by the official managers of the effort to use the arts to win the war as too potentially damaging to national morale. He turned it, therefore, into what he hoped would prove a universalized statement about the outraged response of a free people duped by greedy traitors in their community into leaving themselves too trustingly open to occupation by an enemy force seeking to exploit their resources as part of its plan for world conquest. The problem was one Steinbeck would face again: finding a convincingly universalized setting for a fiction closely paralleling contemporary events (Orson Welles had faced just the opposite problem in 1938 when his radio broadcast of H. G. Wells's *War of the Worlds* too convincingly used realistic settings for fantastic events). Despite Steinbeck's repeated disclaimers, the setting so closely resembled Norway under Nazi German occupation that the novel and play were usually treated as a specific response to an event that had shocked the whole free world, while Steinbeck's implied warning to his own country was ignored. He compounded the problem by writing very fast and leaving in some references that could apply only to the current European situation. Actually, all the protestations were to no point, for the patriotic Norwegians greatly admired the story and rewarded the author generously when they were free again.

American audiences who had anticipated that Steinbeck's first production since *The Grapes of Wrath* (*The Forgotten Village* remained virtually forgotten) would be another epic treatment of another national crisis were annoyed that he should turn to distant events with which they felt no direct involvement. A principal complaint was that the characters were the symbolic types he intended them to be. He was annoyed about such treatment of his good intentions—a gap was widening between him and a public already divided in its response to his earlier successes.

Especially in victimized Europe, on the other hand, the occupied nations viewed the intended tribute an impassioned protest against tyranny. The novel was translated and printed surreptitiously by resistance presses to inspire their fighters' efforts. The odd result was that although Steinbeck was hailed abroad for treating the invaders as a technologically superior force that had won a quick victory but was vulnerable to the guerrilla tactics of a dedicated band of freedom fighters, he was condemned in the United States for not making the Nazis as thoroughly hateful as they should have been in order to whip up public sentiment against them.

The argument that Steinbeck was not familiar with the invaders in *The Moon Is Down* missed his attempt to convey the universality of the ruthlessness of the power seekers. The fault, however, was partly his—or his censorious government superiors'—because in writing the final version he was not able entirely to abandon his original conception. Though he did not have firsthand experience with Nazis or other European authoritarians at that time, he knew and hated the California vigilantes, and he had only to dress them in foreign uniforms, venting some of the wrath he thought he had purged when he destroyed "L'Affaire Lettuceberg" but was never able to repress totally before it was rekindled by his attempt to return to California in 1945.

One lingering evidence of his original motivation occurs in a conversation between some young men preparing to flee the occupied country by boat for England and the brave Mayor Orden, Steinbeck's heroic figure, who eventually accepts death rather than capitulate to the conquerors. Orden asks them to ask the British to drop weapons to them:

> Tom wiped his forehead. "If we get through, we'll tell them, sir, but— well, I've heard it said that in England there are still men in power who do not dare to put weapons in the hands of common people."
> Orden stared at him. "Oh! I hadn't thought of that. Well, we can only see. If such people still govern England and America, the world is lost, anyway."[1]

This sideswipe could have caused some of the resentment against the work in the United States, though it probably was largely overlooked, and it is likely that Steinbeck intended to provide his American town in the original version with a mayor like Orden, as Sinclair Lewis had provided an underground hero when he depicted a fascist takeover in the United States in his novel *It Can't Happen Here* (1935).

The novel suffers from inconsistencies because of the lingering influence of "phalanx" theory that had intrigued Steinbeck in the 1930s, stressing that organized mobs form a phalanx that "has emotions of which the unit man is incapable, " (*Life,* 80). Its influence appears to be responsible for one of the most questionable exchanges in the novel, when Mayor Orden tells the commander of the occupying troops, "In all the world yours is the only government with a record of defeat after defeat for centuries and every time because you did not understand people" (86–87). If the comment is taken to apply to the Nazis, it is inaccurate, for Germany had won in 1871, for example, the war with France that set off the whole pattern until 1945 (but Steinbeck's history was often questionable). The comment seems rather to describe a certain kind of people who tend to lose their individuality in "phalanxes" and thus fail to recognize that "the one impossible job in the world" is "to break man's spirit permanently" (89)—to merge freedom-loving individuals forever into a phalanx. The ambiguity, however, suggests that the circumstances under which the work was produced resulted at times in careless wording.

What the European resistance valued about the work was not Steinbeck's theorizing but the portrait of Mayor Orden, who becomes a martyr to his principles. He does not simply go under like Danny in *Tortilla Flat* and Jim Nolan in *In Dubious Battle,* because he understands exactly what he is doing when an impasse is reached at which death offers the only freedom and dignity. *The Moon Is Down* is by no means a sentimentally optimistic work. Even though the conquered people take heart by picking up the chant "the flies have conquered the fly paper," Steinbeck does not leave the fatuous impression that slogans alone may carry the day. One must understand and accept the possible consequences of one's commitments. Steinbeck would never create in his fiction an American character in a position of authority with such capabilities. It would have been interesting to see what he could have made of his first conception of this novel. His reputation as a creative artist remains based on his "outsider" works. *The Moon Is Down* is a flawed work, but it has a drive and a bite that leave one with more admiration for its compassionate author than its captious critics. It suggests that Steinbeck was not going down without a struggle, even though the rising of his own moon again was no more certain than that of his characters as he leaves them.

Bombs Away: The Story of a Bomber Team

Steinbeck's own moon certainly did not rise with his next project to deal directly with his country's role in World War II by creating a crew of heroes in the making. *Bombs Away* (1942) is his first book best forgotten; still, in his defense it must be pointed out that he did not want to write it. It was an assignment—from the president—to produce a morale-boosting work to acquaint Americans with the training of a bomber crew. The stilted, colorless prose suggests both its official origin and the author's lack of enthusiasm—cheerleading had never been his strongest gift. Although usually cataloged as a nonfictional documentary, it is not. It is a work of fiction on the level of a comic strip. Its characters are not distinctive individuals but two-dimensional types, less interesting than the symbolic figures in *The Moon Is Down*; they provide not Steinbeck's customary isolated hero but a company of brave men. That Steinbeck was still hanging on to the phalanx theory to find something to say about this crew is apparent from his introduction, describing young loafers of the immediate prewar years, while stressing even more than in *Moon* his disenchanted view of those years out of which he had made such capital:

> The young people were not unlike those clots of boys who hang around the fronts of poolrooms waiting for something to happen. An anarchy of thought and action had in fact settled over the young people of the country. An antidote for the poisons of this idleness and indirection might eventually have been found, some great building program for the betterment of the country (some economic direction or trend to tear away the lethargy). But meanwhile, with one set of certainties gone and no new set established, the country floundered about . . . so convincingly that our enemies considered us to be in a dying condition. . . . In attacking us, they destroyed their ally, our sluggishness, our selfishness, and our disunity.[2]

What seems to be setting out as a serious critique of the American psyche quickly turns out, under the circumstances of the assignment, to reach a conventionally propagandistic conclusion: "[T]he bomber crew will have a great role in defending this country and in attacking its enemies. It is the greatest team in the world" (17), and at last, after a lackluster account of the crew's training, "[T]he deep growl of the engines shook the air, shook the world, shook the future" (125)—hardly the familiar voice of the skeptical loner that created the world's memories of agricultural California in the 1930s.

Like the patriotic posters of the period, *Bombs Away* may be dismissed quickly as transient propaganda, but it still marks an important stage in Steinbeck's career because of the slow erosion of the awesome talent that had produced *The Grapes of Wrath* in the manufacture of advertising messages. The sincerity of the work cannot be questioned. Steinbeck donated all proceeds, after having to disentangle some red tape, to the Air Force Society Trust Fund. What is disturbing is whether the jingoistic rhetoric here in response to the president's request was inflating a sense of the possible importance the writer had so much feared.

Lifeboat

A clear answer is not provided by a story treatment he was developing for an Alfred Hitchcock movie—*Lifeboat* (1943)—that can be taken in two ways. Although this study is limited to Steinbeck's published works, an ambiguity about this work exists even in that respect. An effort to publish the text commercially reached even the point of advertising its sale before it was suppressed by his estate in a wrangle over copyright ownership. Despite Steinbeck's wishes, the text is easily available to anyone who wants to see it, and it has been critically analyzed. It is important because it is the major clue to his creative state of mind between the flawed universality of *The Moon Is Down* and his last great book evoked by the lost California of the 1930s, *Cannery Row*. Comparison with Hitchcock's film is little to the point here, since the director eliminated most of the material relevant to the evolution of Steinbeck's fiction, and the author tried unsuccessfully to have his name removed from the screen credits.[3] What it illustrates is an increasing politicization of Steinbeck's views along the line of the brief comments in *The Moon Is Down* and his introduction to *Bombs Away*. Although he had disavowed any interest in the political disputes behind the events depicted in *In Dubious Battle* and eschewed any political solutions to the matters treated in *The Grapes of Wrath* (though not in his earlier stories about the migrants for the *San Francisco News*), Steinbeck evidently had been or subsequently became much more critical of what he considered the federal government's inadequate, fumbling efforts during the depression to devise programs to improve morale and strengthen young people's contributions to the development of the nation than he had wished to appear before World War II.

His criticisms emerge from his portrayal of two of the seven persons who find their way into a lifeboat after their American merchant ship is torpedoed by a German submarine. The thin plot line is provided by the efforts of a German they rescue, whose exact identity is never revealed before he is thrown overboard, to steer them toward a ghostly "raider ship," flying American colors but manned by uniformed Germans. The long haul in the lifeboat, however, provides principally a backdrop for cynical conversations about America's future prospects, quite at variance with the pep-rally rhetoric of *Bombs Away.*

Most striking of the speakers is a personable and sharp-tongued actress who has married a prominent publisher and been elected to Congress—almost surely modeled after Clare Boothe Luce, celebrated for the vixenish Broadway hit *The Women* (1936), who had married Henry Luce, publisher of *Time, Life,* and *Fortune* and a constant critic of Steinbeck. She had later become a Republican congresswoman from fashionable Fairfield County, Connecticut. What Steinbeck thinks of her point of view becomes evident through her conservation with the merchant seaman narrator, whom she tells that she ran for Congress because the Democrats were ruining the country and she wanted to free working people from the control of labor unions. The narrator keeps his thoughts to himself but reflects in his writing that he had heard Democrats say the same thing about President Hoover that she was saying about Roosevelt and that the people who sought to free workers from dictatorial unions were the ones whom the unions had forced to raise wages.

He decides not to bother to tell her a story that her remarks bring to mind—that both rich and poor Americans have the right to starve to death, but the rich rarely take advantage of it. He ends up thinking to himself, in a foreshadowing of *The Wayward Bus,* that the trouble with a woman like this one who doesn't want to stay at home is that something is missing from her home life.

Her male counterpart, who to her displeasure is elected captain of the lifeboat, is a former racing driver who has become president of a firm making war planes. He also thinks that what the country needs is to get rid of the present administration and end relief by getting the factories going. The narrator's only silent reaction is shock at finding that a self-made man with so much money and influence is not at all bright and does not understand the problems underlying the national malaise.

Hitchcock and Twentieth Century-Fox were scarcely likely to circulate such sentiments in a film intended to stimulate win-the-war feelings, although they may also have been perplexed by the narrator's also turning on the working class to observe that the fellows who were sent into the army from the pool room in his hometown (as mentioned in

Bombs Away) just wanted to get back to shooting pool and staying off—
or on—relief. He explains, however, that he does not think anyone in or
out of the army is so stupid as to think nothing is wrong with the country and that what bothers soldiers about taking orders is that they know
there are chiselers in the government but that it has become unpatriotic
to say so.

Such cynicism would become commonplace in the United States after
the war, but in 1943, with the worst fighting still ahead, it would have
been not just unpatriotic but demoralizing. Though it is not clear why
Steinbeck had fallen back into the same cynical mood in which he wrote
In Dubious Battle and "L'Affaire Lettuceberg" after creating a series of
heroic figures, his relations with a government containing elements that
both sought his services and rejected them as possibly subversive were
not likely to have improved his state of mind. Certainly there is no hero
on his *Lifeboat*—even the streetwise narrator is afraid to be too outspo-
ken and simply shudders silently at the ravings of those he despises.
Whatever was responsible for his mood, the story treatment that
Steinbeck finally submitted to the studio had been cut back 86 pages,
about one-third of its length. It must have helped him again get a lot of
things out of his system. His next work was to be in an unprecedented
vein—one that, though short-lived and never revived, produced his most
spectacularly affirmative statement about the potential of the individual.

Chapter Nine

Art for Art's Sake:
Transcendent Man in
Cosmic Monterey

Cannery Row

Not much is on record about the origins of *Cannery Row* (1945). After finishing his exhausting labor on *The Grapes of Wrath,* Steinbeck had turned for a change of pace to a work done purely for fun (*Working Days,* 116, entry 114); it first took the form of a play, to be called "The God in the Pipes." As he thought possible when he started it on 24 July 1940, it was never finished, and he apparently gave it up in 1941. Roy Simmonds, however, believes this is the work to which he returned after having served as a reporter in the Mediterranean battle zone in 1943. In December Steinbeck wrote his friend Webster Street that he was "working on a funny little book that is fun and it is pretty nice" (*Life,* 265)— part of this seems to have been transformed into chapter 8 of *Cannery Row,* about Mr. and Mrs. Sam Molloy and their rented pipes.

In January 1944 he and Gwyn went on vacation to Mexico, where he found—as he had before—that he did not want to do any writing. "I'll get to work on the little book as soon as I get back," he wrote Pascal Covici; "I want it to mellow a little longer" (Benson, 542–43). During this period the idea for *Cannery Row* apparently emerged, as Steinbeck had added that he had devised some new characters. The book itself was written back in New York in six weeks. During the more than five years since completing *The Grapes of Wrath,* Steinbeck had written nothing that advanced his reputation and much that had been sharply criticized. The war had upset his schedule and distressed him, but readers—and his publishers—were beginning to wonder what had happened to him. One thing that benefited *Cannery Row* was the working conditions under which it was written—he worked as he had on *The Grapes of Wrath,* without distractions in a small office at Viking Press, where Covici could keep a close eye on his progress while Gwyn rested at home during her first pregnancy. Near the end of July he won a bet with her by finishing the book just before their first son, Thom, was born.

He revealed something else that greatly affected the composition of the novel when he wrote his old friends Rich and Tal Lovejoy in Monterey that it was "born out of homesickness" and that he planned to move back to California as soon as the baby could travel (Benson, 553). In October the Steinbecks bought a local historic landmark, the Soto House, near the Monterey waterfront. The novel was published in January, and the sales were his best since *The Grapes of Wrath.*

Reviewers objected to such a frivolous work being written while the war was going on, but Steinbeck commented that one reason for writing it was to provide the troops he had met with what they had asked for— something to take their mind off the war. He became especially annoyed by comments that he was repeating *Tortilla Flat.* This annoyance was well justified, because although both works are set in Monterey, are episodic in structure, and prominently involve groups living on the margin of respectable society, they are written from totally different perspectives and focused on totally different central figures. *Cannery Row* is, in fact, a counterpoise to *Tortilla Flat.* As discussed in earlier chapters, *Tortilla Flat* was one of three novels that, though not planned as a tryptych or even in any acknowledged relationship to each other, examined the fate of three dreamers from a heavily ironic modernist vision of the dispossessed and alienated. *Tortilla Flat,* the first written, portrays a wild, anarchic figure who chooses to destroy himself rather than submit to civilized demands, thus ending a vision of community based on an unstable foundation—a forerunner of the "antiheroes" to become familiar after the war.

Doc in *Cannery Row,* quite to the contrary, manages to maintain his individuality and clear vision without being destroyed or forgoing his dream. He faces problems similar to those of Danny, Jim Nolan, and George in the earlier novels, but whereas they were inexperienced, overconfident, unrealistic, and not wary enough, Doc moves cautiously and does not overreach himself. He faces with Frankie, a young spastic who admires and trusts him, the same kind of problem that George did with Lennie, but he is sadly wise enough to recognize that the boy must be institutionalized before it is too late to avoid catastrophe. He does not stake his happiness on diminishing chances of escaping consequences.

Doc belongs to the new group of Steinbeck heroes—Juan Diego of *The Forgotten Village* and Mayor Orden of *The Moon Is Down*—in his dedication to a chosen life of service. Yet he differs from the others in that he does not face the difficult choices of sacrificing his traditional community like Juan Diego in *The Forgotten Village* or his life like Mayor Orden in *The Moon Is Down*. He avoids any political commitment to the group and chooses a life-style that allows him to serve the community as he sees fit. To understand Doc's choice, we must make our way through the novel, as we must through *The Grapes of Wrath* to understand the transformation of the Joads.

Although Steinbeck complained about critics' failure to understand his book, he contributed little to facilitate understanding. (He like J. D. Salinger, always took for granted an affinity with the reader that made his intentions easier to perceive than they often were.) He offered no elaborate explanations of his plans for this work, as he had for *The Pastures of Heaven* and *Tortilla Flat*. What he wrote to his old friend Carleton Sheffield after he had completed the novel is highly personal and not very illuminating to outsiders: "It's written on four levels and people can take what they can receive out of it. One thing—it never mentions the war—not once. . . . You'll find a lot of old things in it. I find I go back to extensions of things we talked about years ago. Maybe we were sounder then. Certainly we were thinking more universally" (*Life*, 273). One thing that this intimate statement does make clear is that the novel was indeed written "out of homesickness," not just for a place but for old associations, lost certainties. Another is that when Steinbeck speaks in chapter 2 of "the hurried mangled craziness of Monterey and the cosmic Monterey where men in fear and hunger destroy their stomachs in the fight to secure certain food, where men hungering for love destroy everything lovable about them,"[1] he is insisting that the story does have on one level universal implications that must be considered.

Two further distinctions between this novel and *Tortilla Flat* will be useful to bear in mind while examining it in detail. First, as the statement to Sheffield stresses, this is a memory novel. Although *Tortilla Flat* begins when Danny comes home from the army—probably in 1919, some years before the writing of the novel—it is a postwar tale of a community still existing (though it has since disappeared) when the novelist was writing. While *Cannery Row*, on the other hand, cannot be precisely dated, 1937 is mentioned as the year the Malloys began renting out pipes, and flagpole skating was a depression-period sales promotion. The absence indeed of any mention of the war in a community full of soldiers and sailors at local bases like Fort Ord during the war indicates that

Steinbeck is trying to recapture the lost community before the war that had permanently changed it. He was also writing not—as he had in the 1930s—about scenes close at hand that he had recently observed but in an office on New York's Madison Avenue about a land remembered a continent away in space during a vanished time. He made this novel from the gifts and punishments of memory.

Second, although the two novels are set on the edges of the same, rather small community, the first presents a landscape and the second a seascape. *Tortilla Flat,* as befits its Arthurian influences, is a novel of going into the woods; *Cannery Row,* a novel of going down to the sea, of the littoral.

The littoral, strictly speaking, is that space between the high-tide and low-tide marks along a coast which in England, for example, belongs to the Crown and may not be blocked off for private use. It may extend to half a mile along the Welsh Coast or be only a few inches wide along the Mediterranean, although especially in regions like the latter the term has been extended to include immediately adjacent areas, as far as tidal changes extend into estuaries. Especially in such regions as the coast of Brittany, where there are semi-islands like Mont-Saint-Michel with part of the mainland at low tide and islands at high tide, the littoral instills a sense of the uncertainy of things, a consciousness of an inability to define phenomena in constant process of change, in defiance of Aristotle's neat prescriptions.

Those who live along the littoral experience the unceasing changing of their habitats with the incessant ebb and flow of the tides. Those who depend on the products of the littoral cannot surrender to the monotony of a fixed daily schedule, for they must constantly change their schedules as shifting conditions demand. Although there is no regular pattern of movement from the particular to the universal in *Cannery Row,* as there is in the alternations from the Joad story to the interchapters in *The Grapes of Wrath,* there is underlying the structure of the later novel what can best be called a tidal movement.

Working only with the text itself, I have previously tried to demonstrate how Steinbeck applied—with some modifications—the structural plan that he used for *The Grapes of Wrath* to this book, but Roy Simmonds's studies of the typescript submitted to the publisher make clear that my speculations were as misguided as I should have supposed, in view of Steinbeck's distaste for repeating himself. From the information available at the time I devised this scheme in 1960, some previously overlooked interrelationships between parts of the novel could be explained; nonetheless, one must come up with something better to appreciate the pattern of the work in its connecting Monterey with the "cosmic Monterey"—one must try to shift with the tides.

The story begins at a still point where the sometimes-hidden land lies nakedly exposed before the ebbing tide begins once more to flow. On the shore a new order has been established, with Mack and the boys—"the Virtues, the Graces, the Beauties" (*Row,* 18) moved into their Palace Flophouse and Grill. The dynamic movement of making waves begins as "everyone's" thought takes shape of really wanting "to do something nice for Doc," the proprietor of Western Biological Laboratory—a man, Steinbeck writes, whose "mind had no horizon—and his sympathy had no warp" (23).

Movement speeds up like the tide rushing across the sands as plans develop for the first miscalculated party that ends disastrously, leaving the littoral strewn with litter and "a black gloom" settling over the Palace as the tide ebbs. In chapter 25 the tide turns once more, and the book progresses, with Doc now in charge of events, to its culmination in the successful party, climax of the cycle—but not an ending, only a new beginning.

Superimposed on this rhythmic framework is not a single story line—as in *In Dubious Battle*—moving with implacable inevitability, but a variety of vignettes of local life, attempting to place the central action in the large context of a montage of various lifestyles in the community.

After addressing the problems of trying to capture the elusive magic of Cannery Row in words, Steinbeck uses five chapters to evoke the area—something of its history and its inhabitants, not just physically but metaphysically in chapters 2 and 4. Chapter 1 introduces Lee Chong—the Chinese grocer, entrepreneur of the area—and his always wary relations with Mack and the boys. Chapter 3 introduces Dora's Bear Flag Restaurant, the local bordello that provides the feminine note in the area, and in chapter 5, most important of all, Doc's laboratory, though he does not yet appear himself.

In chapter 2 the viewpoint behind the book that also links it with most of Steinbeck's work from *The Pastures of Heaven* to *The Winter of Our Discontent* is evoked by the question, "What can it profit a man to gain the whole world and to come to his property with a gastric ulcer, a blown prostate, and bifocals?" (*Row,* 18). The novel is to be a relentless attack on the pretentious middle-class, go-getting American concept of success in comparison with the outsider life-style of those "blots-on-the-town," Mack and the boys, who "avoid the trap."

The novel, however, is no escapist idyll any more than *The Red Pony,* for death haunts chapters 1 and 3 with accounts of the suicides of the former owner of what becomes the Palace Flophouse and Grill and a bouncer at the Bear Flag, who is unjustly rejected as a "pimp" by even the Palace dwellers. Chapter 4 recounts the encounter of a bold boy who is the only one of his gang to dare challenge an old Chinese man who makes his way through Cannery Row every evening at dusk. The audacious boy is left whimpering by the vision of "the definite cold aloneness of the landscape" he sees through the old man's eyes (*Row,* 19).

Most of the rest of the novel relates the secret plottings and frustrated intrigues to do "something nice" for Doc, and the account is frequently punctuated by short anecdotes that have no direct relationship to Doc or party planning. Steinbeck observed to Covici in January 1945 after the reviews appeared, "no critic has discovered the reason for these little chapters" (Fensch, 43).

There has been disagreement—unlikely to be resolved—about just which chapters he had in mind, depending on how strictly one defines what constitutes a digression from the principal plot line, which is by no means so clear in this relatively short novel as in the much longer *Grapes of Wrath.* Most strictly speaking, those which can be read as independent anecdotes not contributing to the effort to honor Doc are chapters 12 (about Josh Billings's tripas), 14 (sailors and their girls), 19 (a flagpole skater), 24 (Mary Talbot's party), 26 (boys from across the tracks), and 31 (a lovelorn gopher). All feature characters who do not appear elsewhere in the novel, and all tell "spoilsport" stories—five of which stress the nastiness or pomposity of the people from the city of Monterey beyond the railroad tracks.

Chapter 24, however, about Mary Talbot's parties, which might be scoffed at as the most sentimentally upbeat one in the book, does not fit into this context. Although the Talbots are not mentioned elsewhere in the book and none of the residents of the Row appear in this chapter, it does relate to the central motif of party-giving; furthermore, given the carefully worked out interrelations between other chapters, it seems unlikely that Steinbeck just threw it in because he liked it. This whimsical episode does have close relationships to two patterns that, although overshadowed by the attention to Doc and Mack and the boys, are important subtexts in a novel that is more complex than has often been recognized.

One of these is the presentation of female characters in the book. Until Ma Joad picked up the jack-handle in *The Grapes of Wrath* and took over management of the family, women—even important characters like

the unnamed wife in *Of Mice and Men*—had been used to precipitate crucial developments in plots that were primarily concerned with the fates
of the male characters. Women had been the focal figures only in short
pieces like "The Chrysanthemums" and "Johnny Bear" and in some
chapters in *The Pastures of Heaven.*

In *Cannery Row* Steinbeck tries to give the women living marginally at
the Bear Flag Restaurant equal importance with the male dropouts as
community benefactors—a predilection for goodhearted prostitutes that
goes back to the Lopez sisters in *Pastures* and surfaces briefly in "The
Murder" and *Of Mice and Men*. Although the plot line demands more
space for Mack and the boys, Dora's girls are shown to be active benefactors to an ailing community in times of distress, whereas the "boys"
provide only a kind of passive model and not a very competent one for
opting out of the ratrace.

Not all the women in the novel, however, are placed on a pedestal for
such ironic reasons. Ambitious middle-class women are treated with the
same scorn as their go-getting husbands when the narrator observes that
Dora "is hated by the twisted and lascivious sisterhood of married spinsters whose husbands respect the home but don't like it very much" (11).
The only woman specifically pilloried, however, is the absent spouse of
the captain who entertains Mack's boys during their frog hunt; she has
been elected to the state assembly, is on the road doing good, and is
described as the kind who "instinctively distrusted and disliked Mack
and the boys" because "they offered ease and thought and companionship as opposed to neatness, order, and properness" (81).

Mary Talbot's role in a novel stressing this dichotomy between the
meanness of lawmaking women and the kindness of lawbreaking women
is unusual because she is neither and the Talbots are the only characters
in the book expecting to start a family, as the Steinbecks were when he
was writing. Although the whole episode could simply be Steinbeck's
interpolated present for the expectant Gwyn, its point may shed light on
his own presumptions about the sexes. While it is usually Mary who tries
to create a cheery atmosphere to keep her husband going, she turns to
him for consolation when the cruel realities of the tooth-and-claw world
intrude upon her fantasies. Women's role appears to be serving men on
whom they are dependent for protection—a conception that plays only
a subsidiary role in *Cannery Row* but may have great importance in
understanding Steinbeck's own problems during a troublesome decade.

The Talbot episode may also serve to clarify another underlying conception, one critical to determining the motives behind a conclusion that
seems imposed on the text. Edmund Wilson in 1940 had supercilio¬ 'y

dismissed Steinbeck as treating his characters too animalistically—a charge that does not stand up under close scrutiny, although Steinbeck had shown unusual compassion for almost subhuman characters like Tularecito in *The Pastures of Heaven* and Lennie in *Of Mice and Men,* whom he portrayed as having been denied some part of their human birthright. Sensitive people like Mary Talbot, however, do not share the cruel instincts of Kitty Casini, as is indicated when Steinbeck has her say, "I know how cats are. It isn't her fault" (*Row,* 142). Other animals lack the uniquely human potential for sublimating their behavior, although some people, like the boy Willard in chapter 26, may fail to develop it.

This potential difference between the human race and the other creatures with whom it shares its habitat is the climactic subject in *Cannery Row,* as it is symbolized in the juxtaposition of the next-to-last chapter 31, about the gopher, and the final chapter, about Doc's behavior after the successful party. The gopher fable suggests comparisons with the turtle chapter (chapter 3) of *The Grapes of Wrath,* but it is very different in important ways. The gopher is much more anthropomorphised as a decisionmaking creature in sentences like "He had to move two blocks up the hill" than the turtle, which is never anything more conscious of its behavior than a land turtle struggling for survival. Its mechanistically determined course symbolizes the survival instinct that also drives the Joads until at the end of the novel they realize their distinctly human potential by choosing to function as part of a community rather than blindly fighting for the survival of their clan blood. The gopher, on the contrary, is deterministically driven to sacrifice security by yielding to a mating instinct fraught with dangers beyond its comprehension.

The gopher does not suddenly turn up at the end of the novel without any foreshadowing. Early in the novel—in the cautionary chapter 4 about the old Chinese man and the presence of terrifying loneliness in Cannery Row—the gopher might be one of the small animals like woodchucks that sit alone by each mound in bleak landscape.

Human beings, however, are capable of transcending this loneliness without yielding to the procreative instinct that ties them to an ongoing clan and throws them into often fatal competition when resources for survival are limited. One method of such survival is presented in chapter 21, after the failed and destructive first party, when a dejected Mack explains to Doc that he had once been married but his wife only got "hurt" from him until she could stand it no longer, so that now he does nothing but clown and "Try to make the boys laugh" (119). But giving up the struggle for survival in "civilized" society to spend one's life escaping through laughter, though it may make one into a "Beauty and Virtue" of the community, does not realize what Steinbeck considered full human potential. The novel must carry on through another party, one that ends in joyous (even if financially embarrassing) success and sets the scene for the final revelation of Doc's kind of self-fulfillment in contrast to the gopher's

This last chapter of *Cannery Row* is one of Steinbeck's most cryptic, but its contrast with the preceding one suggests an interpretation. After Doc finishes cleaning up the leavings of the party, he reads aloud to himself from "Black Marigolds," a work that reduced Steinbeck to tears, a section concluding with a verse beginning, "Even now / I know that I have savored the hot taste of life." As he reads, "white rats scampered in their cages" and rattlesnakes "lay still and stared into space with their dusty frowning eyes" (181). This final contrast embodies the difference between human beings and other creatures. Humans are different because they have the unique capacity, celebrated in the Hindu poem, to preserve and even to re-create their experiences. They need not live a day-to-day existence and forfeit security necessarily for physical affection, as the gopher must. They can survive on the strength of memories preserved in works of art (as Steinbeck was doing in writing *Cannery Row*).

"Black Marigolds" is introduced into the final chapters of the novel not just because of what it *says* (tells) but because of what it *is* (shows)—a symbol of the highest human achievement. Ultimately the novel is about—as hinted from the beginning—learning with the assistance of art to triumph over immediate sensations and surroundings, to move from Monterey to "the cosmic Monterey." In contrast to Doc, William, the unhappy bouncer in chapter 3, is like the gopher—a creature without psychic resources who, deprived of affection, must set about his own destruction. Doc, the survivor, is by no means perfect, but he cultivates perfectibility. He has learned to find compensation for the frailties of human nature and other shortcomings of an imperfect universe (depicted as maturing the young in *The Red Pony*) in what William Butler Yeats called in "Sailing to Byzantium" "monuments of unaging intellect." Doc is a rarer species than those he collects—one of those "wisest" whom Walter Pater celebrates as spending their mortal interval in art and song.

The novel ends with a cosmic celebration (matching the passing carnival just chronicled) of human transcendence of the imperfect natural world through a participation in art for art's sake, epitomized by Doc's reciting "Black Marigolds" to himself while rattlesnakes stare into space. Unlike *The Grapes of Wrath*, *Cannery Row* is not about achieving a sense of human community (for one already exists among the "no-gooders" on the Row if not among the middle-class "do-gooders" across the tracks) but about transcending its imperfections through recollections of sublime artistic achievements. At a time of extreme disheartenment with what he had seen of the cruelty and irresponsibility of warmaking, Steinbeck found an escape back to sanity through a vision of the highest human potential in timeless art.

Steinbeck could not continue to operate in this transcendent mode. The realities of his own life and the postwar world precluded retirement to cosmic Monterey. *Cannery Row* does not even fit into any evolutionary pattern in his fiction. It is a memory novel, like the poem of memories "Black Marigolds" that it celebrates. A need for escape led to transcendence of his previous selves, yet he was not one who could live on private fantasies until even the idea of publication became "a terrible invasion" of his privacy, as it did for J. D. Salinger. Steinbeck was too restless and becoming too politically involved to rest long in the realm of art. If, however, he could not produce more work in the same vein or did not wish to do so, he would not subsequently equal it. His example itself provides an object for contemplation.

It is doubtful that the death of Ed Ricketts, idealized as Doc in the novel, much as it distressed Steinbeck, was responsible for the next shift in Steinbeck's work—from art for art's sake to moralizing about a contemporary reality that increasingly irked him—for this shift had begun even before Ricketts's death, in Steinbeck's first postwar fiction.

Chapter Ten
Searching for a Folk Hero

At three major turning points in his career, John Steinbeck produced works that got out of his system something that had been bugging him and enabled him to move in new directions. After his first published novel, *Cup of Gold* (1929), he shook off the powerful and baneful influence that contemporary romancers like Donn-Byrne and James Branch Cabell had had on him and found his own most rewarding subject matter and style in *The Pastures of Heaven*. After completing "L'Affaire Lettuceberg" in 1938, he destroyed this "smart-alec" attack on hometown folk to replace it with *The Grapes of Wrath,* a testament of faith in the human spirit that made him an international celebrity, for better or worse. The third change after *Cannery Row,* however, was not marked by another advance in his reputation but by what was generally regarded as a distinct falling off in the significance and style of his writing, as he had exhausted his store of personal recollections of the Monterey region in the 1930s and had also, as Roy Simmonds points out "either lost the ability to reproduce the mature style of the thirties or deliberately abandoned it" (*Achievement, 28*). As I have argued in Chapter 2, it is most likely that this change of style was—like the two earlier ones—deliberate moves as part of his restless experimentation. This time, however, the change was for the worse.

Ed Ricketts served as an icon for veneration but not as a viable model for public emulation. For one thing, it is unlikely that the restless Steinbeck, who was becoming involved in sociopolitical affairs, could have long remained an advocate of art for art's sake; for another, it is unlikely that he thought one could have found "hundreds of others" like Doc in every community, as he supposed one could Juan Diegos in Mexico at the end of *The Forgotten Village*. Steinbeck could linger only so long among memories; the urgent need was for a practical savior for a decaying culture, one who could be found among ordinary people of humble origin, like Tom Joad. Steinbeck's survey of the postwar United States, however, apparently did not turn up much, so that he turned once again to Mexico, which promised more because it was less well known to him.

Almost as soon as he finished *Cannery Row,* he started work on *The Pearl.* Although the novelette was not published until 1947, so that its release could be coordinated with that of a delayed film version, it had appeared as "The Pearl of the World" in the Christmas 1945 issue of *Woman's Home Companion*—just a year after *Cannery Row* began to circulate.

The Pearl

Steinbeck based *The Pearl* (1945–47), his first shortwork to be conceived as a novel/filmscript, on a local legend that he had heard in Baja California during his collecting trip with Ed Ricketts and had recounted in *Sea of Cortez*:

> An Indian boy by accident found a pearl of great size. . . . He knew its value was so great that he need never work again [and] in his great pearl lay salvation, for he could in advance purchase masses sufficient to pop him out of Purgatory like a squeezed watermelon seed. . . . He took his pearl to a broker and was offered so little that he grew angry for he knew he was cheated. . . . After a few more visits he came to know that the brokers were only the many hands of one head and that he could not sell his pearl for more. . . . He took it to the beach and hid it under a stone, and that night he was clubbed into unconsciousness. . . . [He] took the pearl from under the stone. Then he cursed it and threw it as far as he could into the channel. He was a free man again with his soul in danger and his food and shelter insecure. And he laughed a good deal about it. (*Log,* 102–3).

The best thing to do with such traditional tales is to leave them alone to make their own cautionary points, and it is hard to see how this one could be improved by being expanded beyond its retelling. It belongs in a collection like James Thurber's *Fables for Our Times* (1940). Steinbeck, however, raised the curiously literal-minded objection that "this seems to be a true story, but it is so much like a parable that it almost can't be." He found the Indian boy "too heroic, too wise. . . . contrary to human direction."

He returned to it, nevertheless, to inflate it into a high-minded lesson for materialistic cultures that certainly could not have been true. He replaces the Indian boy's dreams that seem entirely compatible with his culture with the vision of Kino—an unwed father guided by the songs he hears in his head—that after he finds the greatest pearl in the world, he can use the proceeds from its sale to finance a church wedding, new clothes, a rifle, schooling for his son—what Jack Kerouac's narrator Sal Paradise in *On the Road* calls "white ambitions," for which he abandoned "a good woman" like the Mexican Terry.[1] Ed Ricketts's fear that Steinbeck's enthusiasm for technological progress was out of keeping with rich traditional Indian cultures is realized in this tale that endows Kino with aspirations far more typical of those of the readers of *Woman's Home Companion* in the United States. Kino has no kinship to the ingratiating rascal of the local legend; Steinbeck was not listening closely to his sources, was missing their point—as he had often complained readers had his—and was attempting to exploit their folk-lore in an alien context. He turned the Mexican fisherman into the same kind of middle-class neurotic that he had only recently satirized in *Cannery Row.*

Some critics, notably Tetsumaro Hayashi, have treated the work as an account of spiritual awakening, as, for example, an illustration of the Zen doctrine of *gedatsu,* "total disengagement" from a "magnificent obsession," and *satori,* "awakening" or "illumination." Steinbeck appears to have intended to turn Kino into some kind of universal moral hero, although there is no evidence of his having been particularly influenced by Zen. But the problem in bringing off this work was that the respons-es that inspired Steinbeck's most memorable fiction were not intellectu-al but compassionately emotional. When he did not trust his feelings, the results were artistic potboilers, but when he kept faith with them—especially when he was dealing with cultures other than his own rural, postfrontier, middle-class American one—he was often wrong, as he was when he did not perceive that the Mexican parable he drew on was not—in the terms he used in describing his own *In Dubious Battle*—"realistic" but "honest fantasy." Kino's action in *The Pearl* seems the result not of intellectual detachment but of a fit of pique in an admission of defeat, like the original Indian boy's, yet it is diametrically opposed to Steinbeck's affirmation from his own cultural tradition not long before, in *The Grapes of Wrath,* that "having stepped forward, [man] may slip back, but only half a step, never the full step back" (205). At the end of the *The Pearl* Kino is even further behind than he was before the discov-ery of the great pearl, for his material heritage has been destroyed and he is left with deflated dreams. One must be careful in assessing this *Pearl* and subsequent works not to mistake his intentions for his achievement. The end may prove morally edifying, but the means of reaching it are suspect.

The Wayward Bus

Steinbeck's next novel, *The Wayward Bus* (1947), also began as a tale of Mexico, but for reasons not explained publicly anywhere, he changed the setting to a mythical highway across the Santa Lucia Range in California. He retained, however, a part-Mexican bus driver named Juan Chicoy (probably for his symbolic initials—the novel is loaded with hokey symbolism) as the resourceful hero who completes the kind of journey to self-fulfillment that had ended in defeat in *In Dubious Battle* and *Of Mice and Men* and that had been left unfinished in *The Grapes of Wrath* and *The Moon Is Down* and aborted in *The Pearl*. Since he had expressed great hopes for this tale in its early stages, perhaps he had begun to feel that he did not understand the differences between Mexican and Californian cultures and that he had better move back to familiar ground.

The cargo that the titular bus carries is not the aspirations to freedom and dignity of the oppressed and dispossessed that appeared in Steinbeck's earlier quest novel but an assortment of what he imagined to be representative middle-class American types, from a Congressional Medal of Honor winner to a stripteaser in the traditional national pursuit of happiness. This long-awaited vision of the post–World War II era proved disappointingly banal. What went wrong is best summed up by one of Steinbeck's best-disposed critics, biographer Jackson Benson: "The characters in *The Wayward Bus* are among his least lifelike and convincing" (Benson, 583).

The trouble begins with the first sentence, which plops readers down in the allegorical California community of Rebel Corners, named for "a very proud and very unpleasant" family of Kentuckians who, during the Civil War, seceded their 160 acres from the Union to join the Confederacy. They subsequently "disappeared from the face of the earth," "through pride and a low threshold of insult which is the test of ignorance and laziness" (*Bus,* 3). From here readers join a band of pilgrims to travel across deserts and mountains and through floods to a coastal town named for the Spanish mystic Saint John of the Cross in an old bus with a palimpsest bumper on which the original Spanish legend of "The Great Power of Jesus" is barely readable beneath the single boldly lettered English word "Sweetheart." This bumper tells the story in a nutshell: austere spiritual faith has been supplanted in a self-indulgent world by sickly sweet lovemaking. We are off in a rickety vehicle on a journey to recover our souls.

We are on the same kind of symbolic journey as the sightseers in *The Pastures of Heaven*, but the irony is replaced by Saroyanesque sentimentality. The difference is cogently summed up by Lawrence William Jones, who traces uneasily the increased reliance on allegory and observes that *The Wayward Bus* "has no significantly organized or logical plot beyond the familiar motif of the pilgrimage. Its emphasis is not upon narrative but attitude, not upon social behavior, but upon social types, not upon character but upon caricature."[2]

Those on board include Mr. Van Brunt, a cranky old man on the brink of death; Camille Oaks, a very sexy woman who does striptease acts at businessmen's smokers; Ernest Horton, who as a soldier won the Congressional Medal of Honor but must now earn a meager living selling repulsive trick novelties; Mr. and Mrs. Pritchard, a successful small-business man and his domineering wife; the Pritchards' daughter Mildred, a restless girl born too soon to become a beatnik or a hippie; Norma, another naive, moviestruck waif like Curley's wife in *Of Mice and Men*; and "Pimples" Carson, an adolescent mechanic addicted to cakes and pies as sex substitutes who wants to be called Kit after his hero. The only other important character is Chicoy's wife, Alice, an alcoholic whom he leaves behind to go on a bender that has little relevance to the story but provides the most memorably written scene.

The more perspective distance gives us from the novel, the clearer it becomes that its principal shortcoming—the artificiality of the characters—results from Steinbeck's failure as a prophet to post–World War II American society. Although there is no suggestion of direct influence, his characters seem derived not from close observation of the emerging society but from the already caricatured figures in Sinclair Lewis's novels of the 1920s, especially *Babbitt* and *Arrowsmith*. Steinbeck was writing too fast, too close to the end of the war. Following the surprising suddenness of VJ-Day before the realities of a nuclear age began to sink in, there was a brief period of euphoria, culminating in Truman's surprising reelection, during which Americans widely assumed that since they had done the job right this time there would be a real return to "normality," as the Harding administration in 1920 had called strict American isolationism and business as usual. The boys from *Bombs Away* could go back to the pool rooms.

There was material for a groundbreaking new novel in California's phenomenal growth, its absorption of the migrants of the 1930s and hordes of snowbirds to follow, and the greatly accelerated pace of mechanization, but Steinbeck was not on the scene to observe it. He was back in an East that had not yet been so drastically changed as the expanding West. Steinbeck's novel was based on a preponderantly patriarchal conception of "business" as it was in the American factories of the 1920s and 1930s (not international corporations fattened by cost-plus wartime contracts) and a rigidly censored Hollywood as the dreammaker for naive and inexperienced young people. The idea of superpower Fortress America as policeman for the world never did penetrate his fiction, despite the travels recorded in his journalism—probably a major reason for his career as a fiction writer ending up unimpressively in 1962.

The central conflict in *The Wayward Bus* is between three generations to control the aspirations of youth and shape the country—as it had been in *The Grapes of Wrath*. Old Van Brunt, the representative of the generation of bankers that had dispossessed the migrants and the go-getter businessmen of *The Pastures of Heaven,* is clearly over the hill and as irrelevant as Granpa Joad. The power broker in this novel is Pritchard, a smalltime operator in search of big deals he probably could not handle. Steinbeck's conception of this character reveals his inability to perceive imaginatively a new age propelled by what President Eisenhower would call "the industrial-military complex," and, of course, its controllers would never be caught riding a rattletrap bus. Steinbeck did not have the experience to create characters like the junkpile magnate in Garson Kanin's *Born Yesterday*. The Congressional Medal winner turned peddler of trash and the fumbling Pimples and starstruck Norma are such extreme figures from opposite ends of the spectrum that one gets no idea, for example, of what might have become of Tom Joad in this changed world

Certainly it is difficult to imagine him aged into Juan Chicoy, who flirts with the temptation to abandon his passengers and run away from his dipsomaniac wife but decides instead to carry on with the journey toward the light after apparently solving restless Mildred Pritchard's problems by what may best be called therapeutic fornication. Indeed, Steinbeck's attitude remains in this novel that women's problems are best resolved in the bedroom, while men should be out on the road, keeping the wheels of progress turning toward some glowing spiritual goal that is left phantasmal. His search for a new hero to emerge from humble people failed to provide a credible guide toward a mythical San Juan de la Cruz or anywhere else.

Viva Zapata!

Despite his usual complaints that his work had not been understood, Steinbeck was probably somewhat daunted by the not markedly hostile but just generally uninterested response to *The Wayward Bus*, for this was his last published novel for several years. He was not finished, however, with the matter of Mexico. He had become interested in following up *The Pearl* (which as a film did practically no business at the box office) with another Mexican legend, *Viva Zapata!* (1952), based on a historical figure who had entered into the mythology of that nation's long struggle for freedom and dignity, the martyred revolutionist Emiliano Zapata (1877–1919). Although the film, directed by Elia Kazan, was not released until 1952, Steinbeck had been involved with this project even before writing *The Wayward Bus* and long before attempting a return to the theater with *Burning Bright*. It was the last of his group of Mexican projects and artistically by far the best of them, as well as his most successful in his striving to create a folk hero as he dealt with the idealization of a historical political figure.

Some historians and critics have complained that Steinbeck's Zapata does not accurately portray the Mexican revolutionary leader, but as Robert Morsberger comments, Steinbeck felt that "perhaps the people didn't need a leader, but they need a legend."[3] By creating a mythical hero whose aspirations exceed his achievements, Steinbeck created a counterpart to Mayor Orden in *The Moon is Down*, who is victimized by greedy traitors within his own community. Living men might prove fallible like even Doc in *Cannery Row*, but a legend can be treated only as an inspiration.

Such a figure, however, as Kino in *The Pearl* illustrates, is difficult to fashion in written fiction, which communicates most successfully the internal struggles of an individual to the individual reader. Film, however, presents physical embodiments to be shared as communal visions. The appeal of moving pictures is basically kinesthetic rather than intellectual.[4]

It seems likely that after *Cannery Row*, Steinbeck's stature as an artist might have been greater had he concentrated on film. His cinematic treatment of his own *The Red Pony* is an extraordinary example of an artist reworking his material to meet the demands of a different medium, and the stage directions for *Viva Zapata!*, although Elia Kazan did not always follow them, are written in a clean, lean prose missing from

Steinbeck's fiction of the same period that shows how well he *envisioned* the action, as the creator of successful cinema must.

The effect of the film was also strengthened by Kazan's direction of the intensely charismatic Marlon Brando as the hero. Although critics have objected to the verisimilitude of Brando's performance, he added to the legendary quality of the film by evoking the image of the "outsider" in violent opposition to decadent traditional societies that he had already established in his first two films, *The Men* and *A Streetcar Named Desire.* Brando continues to instill interest in the legend that would not be commanded for most readers simply by Zapata's name.

Unfortunately, the film proved to be Steinbeck's last personal involvement with Hollywood, although he was enthusiastic about Kazan's film based on the final chapters of *East of Eden,* to which he made no contribution. After the years of work he had put into creating an impressive motion picture, the producers became nervous about the reception of what could be regarded as a controversially radical story during the McCarthy era. Although *Viva Zapata!* was well reviewed and has become an art theater classic, it received little promotion and quickly disappeared from commercial theaters. Because the film version of *The Pearl* also received limited distribution to small audiences in the United States, Steinbeck became disgruntled about the prospects of being adequately compensated for his efforts by an industry that many at that time considered on the verge of extinction, as a result of the inroads television had made on mass audiences. He was probably also fed up with long delays in the production of films he was associated with the long-deferred, often disappointing financial returns. He decided to return to the stage to produce what is usually regarded as his worst failure, *Burning Bright,* which despite the glowing title finally chosen for it proved in no way illuminating.

Burning Bright

While the idea that everyone is responsible for all the world's children can hardly be faulted as a theme for a UNICEF fund drive, such moralizing rarely provides a stimulating theatergoing experience, especially after the audience has dined and wined too well. Whether to universalize his message or to increase appeals to varied audiences, Steinbeck decided to use some confusing gimmicks in unfolding his parable. In the first act of *Burning Bright* (1950) the characters are circus performers; in the second, farmers, and in the third, a ship's crew—although they have the same names and relationships to each other as husband, wife, lover, and friend throughout. Also, the second act begins in June and ends at Christmas, though the action is continuous. Steinbeck attempts to prepare the audience for the curious shifts to come by having Joe Saul, the husband and principal character, say near the beginning, "I know it is a thing that can happen to anyone, in any place or time—a farmer, a sailor, or a lifeless, faceless Everyone!" (*Burning,* 16).

The words *lifeless* and *faceless* are singularly unfortunate choices in the context, and the use of universalizing devices succeeded only in confusing theatergoers, some of whom supposed that circus performers must spend part of the year on a farm. One reading the novelette has the uneasy feeling that the action takes to sea in the last act so that the villain, Victor, can be conveniently pushed overboard: his abrupt disappearance would be harder to manage elsewhere. Even Steinbeck himself finally admitted to Peter Lisca that the work was "too abstract" and "preached too much" (Lisca, 211).

Furthermore, when one does look closely at all this preaching, a question arises not just about the clumsiness of the vehicle for its delivery but about the tenor of the message itself. Just what does "every man is father to all children and every child must have all men as father" (108) mean in practical terms? While everyone has some measure of responsibility for the entire human community—as the Joads learn in *The Grapes of Wrath*—the act of fathering creates a special relationship and special responsibilities that cannot be meaningfully extended to the vast population of the world. As Joseph Conrad's Marlow says of Kurtz in *Heart of Darkness,* one hopes that those with a "general love of mankind" will also have "particular" responsibilities. Universal concern can lead to self-deification, as it does in *Burning Bright* in the vigilantelike disposal of Victor after exploiting him. Steinbeck appears to be endorsing the very kind of purely emotional behavior he had earlier condemned, apparently without carefully thinking through what he was doing.

The irredeemable problem with *Burning Bright* was bad planning. The writer who a decade earlier had worked out the magnificent structure of *The Grapes of Wrath,* in which the message is subtly projected through the narrative in the conversation of humble people struggling for survival, had begun "preaching too much" and plotting too little. Many critics ruefully (and some vengefully) observed that Steinbeck was burning out instead of burning bright.

Chapter Eleven

The Last Big Push

Although *Burning Bright* was probably Steinbeck's least satisfying novel, it set a pattern for his remaining fiction. In Joe Saul he had at last created what he obviously considered a humble hero who refuted proud and greedy Henry Morgan's cynical dictum that civilization must split a person who does not go under, a dictum that had guided the shaping of all his previous fiction (even Tom Joad and Doc in *Cannery Row* had rejected civilization by transcending it but sought only to inspire rather than control others). Joe Saul, however, accepts the role of universal patriarch, while villainous Victor is the one who "goes under," all too literally.

Despite its shortcomings, this muddled allegory seems to have induced in the author a mind-set that nurtured a self-confidence that may not produce the most fruitful results for a visionary novelist. As Howard Levant points out in launching his discussion of *East of Eden*, *The Grapes of Wrath* "vanishes in Steinbeck's claims for his new epic: " 'I think everything else I have written has been in a sense, practice for this. . . . If East of Eden isn't good then I've been wasting my time. It has everything in it I've been able to learn about my art or craft or profession in all these years.' " Levant's "more balanced judgment" is that it is "a strangely unblended novel, an impressive, greatly flawed work."[1] Harold Bloom is less balanced and more final with his observation that the novel does not bear rereading. Yet because of the author's sense that this novel is his only one to match *The Grapes of Wrath* in length and scope, it obviously cannot be passed over lightly in reviewing Steinbeck's accomplishment.

Levant's comment about its being "unblended" must relate to Steinbeck's trying to contain in a single work a historical account of his mother's family, the Hamiltons, early settlers in the Salinas Valley (which provided the original title), and a fictional Trask family, vested in heavy Gothic trappings of myth, including biblically portentous names. On some occasions members of these two tribes even meet, producing with straight-faced seriousness verging on pomposity the same kind of effect as that of Lennie's chastisement by a giant imaginary rabbit near the end of *Of Mice and Men*.

Along the way, since nothing with much sensational dramatic impact happens to the Hamiltons, except for one pathetic suicide near the end of the book, the Trask family takes command of readers' attention. While the Trasks lack the pastoral charm of the Hamiltons, they certainly provide enough salacious scandals to shock not just turn-of-the-century Salinas but midcentury judges of the Book-of-the-Month Club.

After suffering greatly from his relations with his querulous father, Cyrus and his wicked brother, Charles, Adam Trask adds to his burdens by marrying a girl named Cathy, who has, unbeknownst to him, incinerated the father and mother she hated by burning down their homestead and driven a guileless schoolmaster to suicide. Even on their honeymoon Adam is cuckolded by his brother, with the result that twin sons are born, in separate sacs, with different fathers. This does not bother Cathy, who abandons all her menfolk and settles down to managing the local whorehouse after she poisons the founding madam.

Although all this occurs in a small town, Adam does not learn for years what is going on while he raises the twins—Aaron, a sweet boy, and Caleb, a mean one—with the aid of a Chinese servant. Lee, who seems to be based on Steinbeck's fond recollections of an excellent Japanese houseboy in the 1930s, also sets the stage for the conclusion of the novel, by summoning a conclave of Chinese servants to learn Hebrew in order to work out the correct interpretation of the term *timshel* in a verse from the biblical book of Genesis about human beings' relationship to sin. It turns out, as Steinbeck discloses in a ponderous explanation that has been disputed by biblical scholars, that the term means "thou mayest," which is taken to mean that humans may choose to avoid sin and thus have free will. Using this gift, Caleb takes Aaron down to the brothel to meet his mother for the first time; the goings-on at her establishment so much shock Aaron that he runs off to join the army and gets killed during World War I, while Cal makes a fortune raising beans. When he tries to give the money to his father, Adam, who has lost a fortune in a pioneering effort to ship fresh lettuce across the country in refrigerated freight cars, it is refused, so that it looks like Cal too is doomed, until Lee recalls to Adam the injunction in the word *timshel* and prevails on him to embrace Cal.

Peter Lisca set the dominant pattern for criticizing the novel in 1958. He was not well disposed toward it, arguing that "there is not the organic relationship between the parts of the novel that there is between the scenic and panoramic sections of *The Grapes of Wrath*." He finds that the heavily stressed "moral philosophy of the narrator . . . at times seems to

be in direct variance with the action," so that the new direction
Steinbeck had taken in this work "had disastrous consequences for his
art" (Lisca, 275).

During the 1960s this verdict was echoed and augmented. Joseph
Fontenrose maintained that the reader is never clear about the message
of the novel, because "the moral is imposed upon the story. . . . [T]he
myth invoked does not adequately interpret the narrated events."[2] Even
the usually cautious F. W. Watt concluded, after providing a useful catalog of the novel's shortcomings, that, approached as "the best fruit of
Steinbeck's maturity," "the novel can only be seen as an anti-climax, a
large, sprawling, discordant narrative, mixing realism, melodrama, semi-
abstract philosophizing, and personal testament."[3]

During the more idealistic mid-1960s, after Steinbeck had received
the Nobel Prize, efforts began to claim greater consideration for the
novel's relationship to Steinbeck's lofty assertions in his speech accepting
the prize. Lester Marks found *East of Eden* "the apex" of a consistent thematic development in Steinbeck's work," as for the first time he went
beyond affirming that man can survive the struggle between good and
evil—"His vision in this novel is of man victorious over evil."[4] Pascal
Covici, Jr., also points out that the novel "explicitly celebrates man as
the creature who can choose between good and evil," but he cautiously
acknowledges that "by turning to the creation of deliberate choosers in a
morally weighted world rather than of mystically integrated seers in a
unified and amoral ecology, John Steinbeck risked his power to make life
upon the page to a greater extent than any other novelist who comes to
mind." Covici avoids a definitive judgment, concluding that "how successful he finally was . . . will become more apparent as the immediacy
of his social issues yields to the long-range relevance of his moral concerns."[5] Lawrence William Jones has been grouped with defenders of the
novel because he seems to reflect Steinbeck's own position when he
begins, "one can easily see this massive parable as the epitome of many
of Steinbeck's methods and beliefs." But this admission leads to a subtle
letdown at the conclusion of Jones's sophisticated analysis when he
insists that "Steinbeck's use of the themes and techniques of romance in
this parable remains experimental" and "the work does not 'rigidly subject itself to laws,' as Hawthorne suggests romances must and in this
respect, it 'sins unpardonably.' . . . It fails to assimilate gracefully much
of its content," (Jones, 28). This is one of the most astute judgments ren-
dered of what Howard Levant called "the author's enduring difficulties

in fusing structure and materials into a harmonious whole." (Levant, 234).

More is involved in these judgments than simply the long-running dispute over the relative importance of style and content to the stature of a literary work, because Richard Astro also adds to the discussion the significant point that the novel fails not just for stylistic and structural reasons but "mainly for the incongruous application of a set of old ideas [which grew largely out of the novelist's friendship with Ed Ricketts] in a novel about man's struggle to choose good over evil" (Astro, *JS&R*, 211–12), by resorting to the "non-teleological method to prove a restrictive teleological thesis—a convenient approach perhaps, but one that is not philosophically satisfying" (210). The discussion seemed to rest at this post when, in the revised edition of *John Steinbeck*, I concluded that despite his ambitions, Steinbeck "remained essentially a Naturalistic writer who was more successful in portraying sympathetically the confused and defeated than in dramatizing intellectual solutions to moral dilemmas."[6]

The principal subsequent effort to justify greater critical respect for *East of Eden* was made in 1979 in a panel on "Mapping *East of Eden*." Daniel Buerger commends Paul McCarthy's then recent study of Steinbeck for treating the novelist without condescension, but McCarthy sums up his account with the equivocal statement that "If the insights into good and evil reveal no unusual depths or subtlety, they do show a complexity seldom evident in Steinbeck's earlier works"[7]—hardly high praise and again focused more on intentions than achievement. Buerger goes on to list a number of still needed studies—like Steinbeck's use of "musical counterpoint, tempo, and rhythm"[8]—without dealing with questions of the effectiveness of his rhetoric.

Wayne Booth's phrase "rhetoric of fiction" is to the point here, since the bulk of the most carefully considered responses to *East of Eden* are summed up by Louis Owens's explanation that in *The Grapes of Wrath* "Steinbeck is a moralist by implication, but in *East of Eden* he becomes an explicit moralist, and in so doing he loses touch with the power of his finest writing, the power of presenting detail that generates its own moral" (*Re-vision*, 154–55).

Even Owens's well-made point, however, does not quite specify what the "everything" was that Steinbeck said he had learned about his work and had put into *East of Eden*. He had something very explicit in mind about this problem of implied and explicit morality in a letter he wrote to Covici from Nantucket on 11 September 1951, while he was working on the novel: "I have been trying to think how long it is since a book about morality has been written. That is not to say all books are not about morality but I mean openly" (*Life*, 429).

He should have stopped short and wondered why he could not think of any such books. Plenty were being written and published. Lloyd Douglas's *The Big Fisherman*, to cite only the most conspicuous example, had been the best-seller in 1948. Steinbeck would hardly have wanted to concede, however, that he was now competing with the author of *Magnificent Obsession*, although he could have used that title appropriately for this book. Overt morality is rarely artful.

Steinbeck had grown impatient with readers and critics missing his points, so that he resorted to preaching, only to lose the audience that was discovering the subtlety of his best works. Besides essentially talking down to his audience, as the overt moralizer must, in his enthusiasm he apparently failed to realize that the two narratives he was attempting to juxtapose did not complement each other for another reason than that one was pastoral history and the other Gothic fantasy.

These two seemingly antipathetic forms can on rare occasions be juxtaposed when the author envisions precisely the reason for the contrast, as William Faulkner does in *Light in August*. But Steinbeck had not found the recipe. He appears not to have considered, as critics have observed, the imbalance resulting from the final emphasis on the twin Cal, although he does not figure prominently in the long narrative until the final section. (By basing his film on this section. Elia Kazan made it a much more climactically organized work than its source; even so, film cannot just jog along over an uneven terrain without losing viewers as happened with ABC-TV's television adaptation of the novel in 1981.)[9]

In the novel, the *timshel* episode is imposed on an already completed story built around two apparently contrasting plots that both come to pathetic conclusions in suicides. The Hamilton family story, when its minor current surfaces occasionally, is a classical Arcadian pastoral that Steinbeck had begun the major phase of his career by depicting as undermined by twentieth-century American materialism in *The Pastures of Heaven*. The Arcadian myth is not, though, about the unalloyed triumph of romantic escape in the pleasures of nature, for as the motto of the death's head in Arcadian painting with the inscription *et ego in Arcadia* indicates, death is always indeed an imminent presence—as Andrew Marvell warns in "To His Coy Mistress"—where time seems gratifyingly suspended.[10]

The world of the Hamiltons—like the tenant farming system in *The Grapes of Wrath*—is doomed from the beginning by a shift from agrarian to mercantile values in society: exactly what the southern agrarians were protesting with greater authority in the decadent South. It is difficult to counterpoint a pattern of broad cultural change of this kind with the hermetic compulsion of an antisocial figure like Cathy Trask, whose motives her creator finds inscrutable but who is ultimately doomed to end in self-destruction like that which overtakes Danny in *Tortilla Flat*. Her story is not even in the naturalistic tradition of Faulkner's Snopes saga; it is rather straight out of the traditional fairy tales of wicked witches, another but quite different survival from pastoral societies that attributes the loss of Arcadia not to natural but to supernatural sources—very probably the kinds of tales that an imaginative young John Steinbeck dreamed up to scare neighbors in a dark basement. The roots of the Trask story may go farther back into his learning his craft than has been recognized. *East of Eden* may be an unblended melange because Steinbeck tried to crowd in too many collective memories without the discriminating selectivity he achieved in *Cannery Row*.

Both the Trask and the Hamilton stories have ended before the climax of the novel in the confrontation between Adam and Cal, with the crucial suicides of Tom Hamilton and Cathy (now Kate). If a novel were constructed to lead to the climactic juxtaposition of the two suicides, it could be an ironic modernist fable portraying how reenactments of two traditional myths of pastoral decadence would come to the same bleak end in the middle-class commercial world that Steinbeck detested, whether one tried to live a good life, as the Hamiltons did, without splitting before the onrush of civilization, or one deliberately chose a career of self-indulgent alienation. What would prove, however, to be an overinflated *Pastures of Heaven* is not what Steinbeck sought two decades later. Wishing to acquaint his sons with something of his past, he hoped to come up with contrapuntal accounts of past failures that would provide a background for future triumphs.

This is a great deal to try to accomplish in one novel, especially if the author neither gives some suggestion of the way it is headed from the beginning nor succeeds in involving the historical, somewhat autobiographical plot meaningfully in the conclusion. The result is that the Hamilton family episodes, which are the best written in the novel, seem to serve no real purpose except to disrupt occasionally the progress of the kind of moralizing Gothic fable that less gifted artists were grinding out regularly.

Steinbeck had originally conceived of his Salinas Valley project as two novels, and possibly the first part of a more successful venture would end with the suicides of Tom and Kate, leaving the situation of agrarian California where it stands at the end of *The Red Pony* cycle, viewed from the wistful, mature viewpoint of *Cannery Row*. The second could then work out against a more complex, relevant background the relationship between Adam and Cal in an expansion of an older Steinbeck's revised approach to *The Red Pony* in the film version. But such speculation is idle indeed, for the literary legacy Steinbeck left his sons owes much less at last to the changing Salinas Valley of the original title than to the biblically fired fantasies of an author who was becoming an increasingly strident preacher.

Chapter Twelve

Ulysses's Final Quests: Cannery Row Revisited, Paris, and Long Island

After completing the monumental *East of Eden,* John Steinbeck was again exhausted, and this time, for the first time in his career, he had to make drastic revisions in his original at the behest of his publishers, dragging out the task far beyond his intentions, as he fretted to get away, like his favorite literary character, Tennyson's Ulysses, in search of "that untravell'd world, whose margin fades / For ever and for ever when I move." As he had after finishing *The Grapes of Wrath,* he sought a change in some lighthearted scene and turned to the notion of making a musical comedy from *Cannery Row* in collaboration with his friend the composer Frank Loesser (*Guys and Dolls*), a project he thought would prove great fun (*Life,* 459).

He quickly found the idea unworkable, however (probably because in his didactic phase he was out of touch with the melancholy that infused the original), and he was prevailed upon by the potential producers to build a new work around the character of Doc, this time featuring a love story and whatever new characters were needed. He decided, Jackson Benson reports, that "the best thing to do would be to make it into a novel and then he or someone else could adapt the novel to the stage" (Benson, 740).

Sweet Thursday

Frank Loesser dropped out along the way, and Oscar Hammerstein finally wrote the script, as well as the lyrics for Richard Rodgers's songs. Steinbeck was enthusiastic about *Sweet Thursday* (1954), informing his agents, "It is kind of light and gay and astringent. It may even say some good things," though he admitted it might be "a little self-indulgent" (*Life,* 473). Reviewers simply dismissed the thin tale as further chapters for *Cannery Row,* proving principally that they did not understand the earlier work, which was entirely different in tone and viewpoint.

Cannery Row had depicted Doc as a person whose mind had no horizon and who transcended the limitations of human life through ecstatic communication with great works of art. The apprehension of such a possibility had, however, been only transient for Steinbeck, and after completing his memory novel he had set off again on the quest that began with the making of Tom Joad—that for admirable models of social progress.

If he were to return to the now distant figure of Doc as metamorphosed from Ed Ricketts, he now felt compelled to adapt the character to a new program that had been beginning since *The Wayward Bus:* to narrow the concept of progress to social adjustment, trying his hand at his first conventional boy-meets-girl story by depicting Doc's hesitant transformation from a lonely, dissatisfied scientist suffering writer's block in his sterile professional studies into a swain infatuated with a reformed prostitute, once his doubts about such a pairing are overcome by her nursing him after his arm is deliberately broken by Hazel, the retarded member of the Palace Flophouse boys retained from *Cannery Row.* Doc and Suzy ride off into the sunset to a lucrative job at a research institute, wangled by a cranky philanthropist named old Jinglebollocks, apparently based on Daddy Warbucks from the "Little Orphan Annie" comic strip, leaving Cannery Row apparently to the tourists whom Steinbeck's work had attracted there.

Critics who had been following Steinbeck's work were not just disappointed but shocked. Peter Lisca speculated that by degrading Doc, Steinbeck, who had used Ricketts as a mask for the authorial point of view in every novel from *The Pastures of Heaven* to *Burning Bright,* could be "modifying that mask to make it a closer expression of his present attitude, . . . which certainly would have been disapproved by the original Doc" (Lisca, 282), although Lisca would subsequently take the book less seriously and simply dismiss it as a musical comedy libretto. Joseph Fontenrose made perhaps the only criticism the novel warrants when he observed that "the attempt to combine the humorous tone of *Cannery Row* with the street's new look is singularly unsuccessful," because the farce "often degenerates into tasteless slapstick" as Doc becomes "good husband and organization man" (Fontenrose, 128).

The novel cannot be quite so simply dismissed, however, because Steinbeck apparently thought that there was something of more than passing entertainment value in the work. Elaine Steinbeck has unequivocally denied that John "set out to demean Ricketts" (Astro, *JS&R*, 195). John himself warned that the musical comedy libretto needed changes, but was ignored; finally, he wrote to Elia Kazan (undated and not published until 1984) that "what really is the trouble is that Rodgers and Hammerstein seem to be attracted to my kind of writing and they are temperamentally incapable of doing it" (Benson, 781).

Richard Astro agrees with earlier critics that the Doc of *Sweet Thursday* "is not only unlike the Doc of *Cannery Row*, but his behavior sharply conflicts with that of his real-life prototype." But he goes on to argue that neither is the work the kind of "cheery affirmation" it has been called, as it reflects "deepseated despair"—"the novelist's dirge over the destiny of the Ricketts-like character in the modern world" (Astro, *JS&R*, 195–99). Mack in the novel observes that everything has changed in Cannery Row's and indeed after the appearance of Steinbeck's earlier novel, Ricketts found it difficult to work there because of the constant stream of gawking tourists. Steinbeck may have felt some sense of regret and culpability for bringing the upwardly mobile middle class that he satirized in the novel thronging into the area. His complaint about the musical comedy version, *Pipe Dream,* was that Rodgers and Hammerstein had not taken a "tougher, more realistic line than they had before" (Benson, 781).

Steinbeck seems to have had in mind something like the rowdy, cynical attack on a meretricious society in Bertolt Brecht and Kurt Weill's *The Three Penny Opera,* which was enjoying an enormously successful revival in a rejuvenated off Broadway theater in Greenwich Village when his novel appeared. Lotte Lenya might have done something with his material that former Metropolitan Opera star Helen Traubel could not, but black comedy was not Rodgers and Hammerstein's forte—they conceived the work as exotic escapism, like *South Pacific* or *Flower Drum Song.* Frank Loesser might have been able to bring off what Steinbeck wanted, for the material was akin to that provided by the raffish characters on the social fringe in his *Guys and Dolls,* and it would be helpful to know more about his dropping out of the project.

Not all of the blame for what Peter Lisca justifiably condemns as the anti-intellectualism of the vehicle can be blamed on Rodgers and Hammerstein. Steinbeck was responsible for the snide tone of the original, which lacks the vivaciousness and cheeky sophistication of the genre fostered by John Gay's eighteenth-century *The Beggar's Opera,* the model used by Brecht and Weill. The putdown of pompous hypocrisy in *Sweet Thursday* is more like backwoods American moralizing than urbane character assassination. Although Steinbeck had the delusion about this time that he had become a New Yorker, the Broadway crowd he hobnobbed with were already concentrating on spectacular tourist attractions, and he apparently did not fit in with the new culture celebrated in the *Village Voice* (founded in 1955). He was still a visitor from the provinces, with conceptions of fiction that depended more on reviving the past than exploring the present. *Sweet Thursday,* however straight or ironically one may take its title, was not "sweet" enough for consumers of popular romances or big box office musical comedies; nor was it tough enough for the just emerging counterculture of the beatniks or off-Broadway theater. The best that can be said for it is that once again Steinbeck was getting something out of his system, but even less successfully than in most postwar productions.

The Short Reign of Pippin IV

One thing that he did get out of his system with *Sweet Thursday* was nostalgia for a vanished California. That was his last visit to the traditional Steinbeck country. The state plays a brief role in his next novel, *The Short Reign of Pippin IV* (1957), but only in mentions of the "chicken capital" Petaluma, in Marin County, north of San Francisco, far from the scenes of his growing up.

He felt ready now to tackle the big city but, significantly, not New York. Although he had now lived there for a decade, he probably quite wisely resisted suggestions from his agents and publishers to tackle the unfamiliar problems of the dispossessed; nor did he hurry his work. Undoubtedly wounded again, by the unkind reception of *Sweet Thursday,* he did not get around to another novel until 1956, when he settled on a story that was set in Paris and had occurred to him while he was living there with Elaine and his sons in 1954.

Much of the action of *The Short Reign of Pippin IV* is set in the house the Steinbeck's had rented at One Avenue de Marigny, across from the Presidential Palace, which had been servants' quarters for a Rothschild mansion next door. Here resides Pippin Heristal, an amateur astronomer who, as a descendant of Charlemagne, is pretender to the throne of France. During one of France's frequent political crises after World War II between the resignation of Charles de Gaulle and his return to power, one attempt to restore stability is made by restoring the monarchy, which proves for a time a tourist attraction.

Pippin, however, begins to take his job seriously and proposes needed reforms. Riots follow, and he is deposed and outlawed, but he returns contentedly to his stargazing. Tempted by power, he refuses to "split" by playing into the hands of manipulators, yet he retains his integrity, proving the true hero that Steinbeck had long sought to create, who asks nothing for himself but to be left to his harmless pleasures exploring the heavens.

It is, unfortunately, difficult to consider this amusing and heartwarming tale as serious literature, because the improbable situations and two-dimensional characters make it resemble most nearly the political cartoons for which the French are famous, especially the wickedly witty ones in *Le Figaro,* to which Steinbeck contributed some articles on an American's impressions of Paris while in residence—something more likely to divert audiences weary with wrangling than to provide any constructive criticism about a political situation Steinbeck grasped only superficially.

Because of his short and sheltered residence, he had never penetrated very deeply into the French psyche. Although the setting is Paris, Pippin's program was obviously constructed to pronounce Steinbeck's idealistic but conventional views as a Stevenson Democrat for solving American problems during the complacent Eisenhower administration:

> The first section dealt with taxes—to be kept as low as possible and to be collected from all.
> The second, wages—to be keyed to profits and to move up and down with the cost of living.
> Prices—to be strictly controlled against manipulation.
> Housing—existing housing to be improved and new construction to be undertaken with strict supervision as to quality and rents.
> The fifth section called for a reorganization of government to the end that it perform its functions with the least expenditure of money and personnel.
> The sixth considered public health insurance and retirement pensions.
> The seventh ordered the break-up of great land holdings to restore the wasted earth to productivity.[1]

The principal shortcoming of this attractive fable is that—like editorial cartoons—it has dated quickly. After only a few years annotations would have been needed to make fully comprehensible gentle satires of once celebrated writers like Françoise Sagan, whose internationally adored romance *Bonjour, Tristesse* has generally been forgotten. Except for the droll invented figures who roam through it, *Pippin IV* really belongs in the account of Steinbeck's journalism rather than his serious fiction.

The Winter of Our Discontent

Steinbeck was clearly slowing down as a fictionist, although his reporting was markedly increasing to develop into a second career. Four years elapsed after *Pippin IV* and before *The Winter of Our Discontent* (1961) appeared—the longest period between novels since the beginning of Steinbeck's career, and this novel was to be his last.

Around the beginning of March 1960, after recovering from a hospitalization, he went back to a satiric short story, "How Mr. Hogan Robbed a Bank," that he had dashed off in 1956. He used this earlier work as a jumping-off point for what was to be his only story of the littoral of Long Island, where he had finally established himself at Sag Harbor after a decade of wandering to find a replacement for the Monterey peninsula.

Like *The Pearl, The Winter of Our Discontent* testifies to the dangers involved in tampering with originals, even one's own, although Steinbeck had earlier been most successful in adapting *The Red Pony* for a new generation and a new medium. The smug, zany Mr. Hogan of the short story is converted into Ethan Allen Hawley, also a grocery clerk, but with many more problems, principally because as a descendant of one of the town's leading families, he had once owned the store. While his plans to rob a bank are introduced somewhat pointlessly into the novel, he realistically abandons them even before he discovers that modern protective devices would have foiled his attempt.

"How Mr. Hogan Robbed a Bank" is a far more enjoyable and craftsmanlike work than *The Winter of Our Discontent,* arguably his last piece of fiction worth keeping in print—as it has been, in the latest version of *The Portable Steinbeck.* It indicates what should have become increasingly clear during his career that his greatest talent was for the vignette—a short, intensely concentrated piece that fits Poe's prescription for the proper construction of a tale. His best work—*The Pastures of Heaven, The Red Pony, Of Mice and Men, The Grapes of Wrath, Cannery Row*—are all episodic or structured in theatrical scenes; only *In Dubious Battle* is a conventional narrative of any length without serious structural problems.

The puff on the cover of the first paperback edition describes *Winter* as "the novel of an honest man's struggles with the seductive temptations of today's easy money and morals." The statement is accurate as far as it goes, but it suggests that the novel treats this difficult issue in some depth. It does not. No five levels can be found here.

Steinbeck concludes in this novel his quest for a fictional hero for contemporary society. Instead of pressing on from Pippin Heristal, however, to fashion some American equivalent of this man who refuses to split or go under and instead turns his back on a self-seeking society to preserve his integrity, Steinbeck swings all the way back to *The Pearl,* his previous effort to turn into a testimony to long-suffering family solidarity this cynically witty fable about a person who transcends an entrapping society by forgoing its temptations.

Hawley, named after Vermont's revolutionary war hero, still lives in his great-grandfather's fine old house on the most fashionable street in town but has lost his place in local society, after his father has lost his patrimony through bad investments and he himself has proved an incompetent businessman by losing the small grocery store he has taken over with his last resources. He is reduced to serving as a clerk in the same store, now operated by an Italian immigrant who is a craftier businessman. Chided by the banker, whose family had been his family's partners and probably responsible for burning their last ship for the insurance when the age of sailing ships ended, Ethan schemes to improve his family's lot for the benefit of his son and daughter.

In the course of this effort, he devises the same kind of tricky scheme to rob a bank in which Mr. Hogan succeeded and rewarded his son, who had won honorable mention in an "I Love America" contest, and his daughter, who was a good sport about her brother's success, with $5 each. In the novel, however, Ethan abandons the unworkable scheme, and although the incident of the son's winning the contest is retained, this time the daughter exposes his having plagiarized. Ethan instead improves his position by winning back the grocery store by informing the immigration service that his employer is an illegal immigrant. When the tired employer decides to retire to Italy, he sells the store to his devoted clerk at a bargain price. Ethan raises the necessary money by beating the banker and his cohorts to the only good piece of land for an airport when it is willed to him by a longtime friend whom he provided with the money to drink himself to death.

When Ethan returns home after learning of his son's disgrace, he finds that the boy has beaten up that "stinking sneak," his sister, for just doing what he tells his father "everybody" does—that's "the way the cooky crumbles."[2] Ethan then goes off to a cave between the tide lines

that has been his secret hiding place since childhood. He plans to go out
with the next ebb tide, but as he reaches for a razor blade to slit his
wrists he finds instead a family talisman whose secrets he has shared with
his daughter. He realizes that her only interest has been to protect her
brother, and that he must return this talisman to its new owner "else
another light might go out" (298).

The change in the novel from the earlier story was just like that made
in dealing with the legend of *The Pearl*—a tale of beating a greedy society at its own game by just taking one's chances for survival has been
turned into a sentimental tale of forgoing self-gratification in an already
compromised situation. Splitting has become the approved course.

Again Steinbeck's intentions cannot be faulted, but has he devised a
moral fable that makes them significant for contemporary society in the
manner of those brought out through the Joad family story in *The Grapes
of Wrath*?

The most successful feature of the novel is Steinbeck's evocation of
the new setting. He was tremendously sensitive to environments like the
Long Island littoral, which must have reminded him of the Pacific
beaches he had left behind. In the most memorable passages of the
novel, he evokes the changing of the once thriving waterfront after the
decline of the trading days of the sailing ships as the once busy dock
areas silted up. Although the novel is set in New York State, it is often
understandably mistaken for a New England story, for the old ports on
northeastern Long Island, far from the crowded city, have long been
associated with those of the lower New England coast and the offshore
islands, Martha's Vineyard and Nantucket, where Steinbeck wrote *East
of Eden*. After a long period of decay, this region was undergoing, during
Steinbeck's residence, the same kind of affluence from a growing tourist
trade that had destroyed the Tortilla Flat and Cannery Row he had
known.

He had not become so familiar with his new society, however, as with
its setting. His concern in the Monterey novels had been with outsiders
who lived marginal lives on the littoral or in the woods, alienated from
the upward-striving middle class across the railroad tracks and in close
touch with a subtly changing natural world. If an "outsider" community
could have maintained itself in Steinbeck's new home during the harsh
Atlantic winters, he was not in touch with it. Circumstances had
imposed on him the enforced privacy of a middle class always notably
slow to welcome newcomers.

He had never felt comfortable with bankers and storekeepers, and
even though he had become much more social than formerly in New

York, he still associated mostly with other writers and theatrical people and never became involved with the middle-class commercial community. The figures in his last novel seem as drawn from literary sources, rather than everyday experiences, as those in his first romance.

He was more at home on Long Island than in the city, because society was still more old-fashioned there than in the city, although as he did perceive, it was changing. But he was again running into the same problem he had encountered immediately after World War II in *The Wayward Bus*—his picture of New Baytown society seemed in the 1960s much like that in Sinclair Lewis's novels of the 1920s and 1930s (even the subplot concerning Hawley's son's plagiarism recalled a scandal in a contest sponsored by Eddie Cantor on his radio program back in 1936).

New Baytown's lagging behind the times is demonstrated by the principal community struggle dramatized in the novel: the effort to find a suitable place for a local airport, a problem the now dominant communities in the country had faced a generation earlier. Steinbeck may well have been reaching especially for readers in those areas which were just being affected by such problems and for which he could still see a greater possibility of a moral recovery. But the problem with the novel in terms of the contemporary society he was addressing was that the moral problems he stresses, the things that "everybody's doing"—employees cheating small-business people, a schoolboy's plagiarizing in a fatuous media contest, profiting from a friend's suicidal tendencies—had been overwhelmed in the turbulent 1960s by the urgency of issues perhaps no more morally significant but on a far greater scale—racism, terrorism, the threat of nuclear disaster—exceeding even the migrant problem faced in *The Grapes of Wrath*. An artist of international stature is expected to contemplate such issues.

Steinbeck's failure, for whatever reasons, to adjust his vision to a changed world can best be suggested by the difference between his treatment of middle-class dilemmas in *Winter* and that of one of the few writers to be received enthusiastically by the largely postliterate "hippie" generation of the 1960s in a novel—ironically, also from Steinbeck's publishers—that did receive the kind of attention that his had had in the 1930s. Ken Kesey in *One Flew over the Cuckoo's Nest* depicts Chief Bromden's waking up to contemporary reality after living many years in a fog as he observes "a train stopping at a station and laying a string of full-grown men in mirrored suits and machined hats, laying them like a hatch of identical insects, half-life things coming pht-pht-pht out of the last car, then hooting its electric whistle and moving on down the spoiled land to deposit another hatch [while the guys went home to] five thousand houses punched out identical by a machine. . . . The houses looked so much alike that, time and time again, the kids went home by mistake to different houses and different families. Nobody ever noticed."[3] People have become too dehumanized to make value judgments, even to perceive individual differences.

Compared with such a vision, Steinbeck's last novel, like *Pippin IV,* seems quaintly old-fashioned—not in the sense that Steinbeck would approve in *America and Americans* (1966), of stressing traditional values, but rather in the sense that they treated as contemporary society one that existed only in scattered parts of a country troubled not so much by smalltime chicanery as by mass robotization.

Steinbeck's old-fashioned response to a global issue emerges in his treatment of the environmental preservation movement in *America and Americans.* In this last major statement that he published on the national culture, he condemned the waste of resources as "evils that can and must be overcome if America and Americans are to survive"—commendable sentiments—but went on to say that "the river-polluters and air-poisoners are not criminal or even bad people" and described the communal response to a man who had destroyed a stand of ancient redwoods as "looking away, because we were ashamed of him."[4] Such comments reflect the nineteenth-century faith in moral suasion, a doctrine holding that people will behave properly to avoid community ostracism, a concept that has never worked very well and certainly has yet to be confirmed as ecological crises mount. Steinbeck was taking a bold and determined stand by abandoning a modernist sense of alienation for a preaching of traditional morality, but he did not come up with a very practical alternative for maintaining the position he had achieved.

Curiously, Steinbeck in *The Grapes of Wrath* had depicted the kind of dehumanization that many writers, from the 1920s on, viewed as the greatest threat to the future of human society in his portrait in chapter 5 of the tractor driver who is wrecking the tenants' homes: "The man sitting in the iron seat did not look like a man; gloved, goggled, rubber dust mask over nose and mouth, he was a part of the monster, a robot in the seat" (48). He was not to pursue this fearsome image, however, though it became ever more relevant to his society. The writers who did seemed to await Apocalypse, and he appeared unable to face that grim prospect.

His turning after *Winter* exclusively to reporting suggests at least that immediate realities were all Steinbeck cared to cope with. He was unable to come up with another story that would embody an imaginative vision worth communicating. What must be said for him is that he, unlike some contemporaries, was not satisfied to simply sit back and scowl at the world. He remained true to the end to Tennyson's vision of the ever-questing Ulysses, and it is really nobody else's business what he should or should not have written. One's business may well be, however, to choose what one wants to read and to recommend to others, so that it is perhaps with regret that one must say that after sharing his memories of his pre–World War II world in *Cannery Row*, Steinbeck did not produce any fiction of significant value in understanding society after that war.

Chapter Thirteen

Steinbeck 2000

Although John Steinbeck won both popular and critical acclaim internationally for *The Grapes of Wrath* just before the outbreak of World War II in 1939, he received only scattered critical attention for the next two decades until 1957, when Peter Lisca's *The Wide World of John Steinbeck* was greeted with a front-page review in the *New York Times Book Review* and established the starting point for critical overviews of this author who would publish only one more novel before being awarded the Nobel Prize in literature in 1962. Only three short introductions to his work—one from England—were added before his death in 1968, followed by two more in the early 1970s.

His neglect is somewhat accounted for by a decline in the popularity of his fiction during the activist years in the late 1960s, when he turned to reporting and became a strong supporter of President Lyndon B. Johnson. But a more valid reason for a lack of new approaches was a paucity of information about this author who disliked personal publicity. The field began to open when in 1973 Richard Astro approached him through the medium of a friend in *John Steinbeck and Edward F. Ricketts: The Shaping of a Novelist,* and a selective *Life in Letters* by his widow, Elaine, and Robert Wallsten shed considerable light on the intentions of his stories. Only the publication of Jackson J. Benson's biography, however, would provide an adequate context for studying his career, and even his 1000-page account has required supplementation, as new material continues to come to light. Still, Steinbeck's destruction of many letters and manuscripts throughout his career leaves gaps that are unlikely to be closed in an understanding of his intentions.

Much of the discussion of Steinbeck, even a quarter-century after his death, has focused on an unquestionable decline in the artistic effectiveness of his fiction after World War II, despite wide admiration of the attitudes it expresses. Such a preoccupation was understandable while he was still alive and publishing, eligible for high honors and having an influential voice in world affairs. But as our perspective lengthens and it becomes ever more strikingly clear that none of the American novelists to win significant recognition for their prewar work gained in stature by that produced after 1945, Steinbeck's position is confirmed as a representative of a particular, distinctive, and disastrous period in human affairs when a worldwide depression drove desperate people into fanatically seeking panaceas in authoritarian utopias. It is enough to say that after 1945 he failed to equal the vividly compassionate responses to immediate experience or its recollection he had earlier evoked. The important matter for the future is to focus on his significant achievements and consider whether they are relevant to changing audiences and how they speak to them about universal human experience.

Steinbeck has always been a particularly challenging subject for such examination. If, as Harold Bloom argues, he is "not one of the inescapable American novelists of our century," we must contemplate why one is yet compelled "to be grateful" for *The Grapes of Wrath*. Such a position renders even agreement about a later decline irrelevant, because a falling off of one's later works is no necessary reflection on the earlier.

One may not entirely agree with Bloom in singling out as his best only three of Steinbeck's early novels—*In Dubious Battle, Of Mice and Men,* and *The Grapes of Wrath*—or with Steinbeck's publishers in adding *Cannery Row* and *East of Eden* to a series of modern classics, for sales records have undoubtedly entered into the calculations. I would like to see *East of Eden* replaced by *The Pastures of Heaven,* accompanied by *The Red Pony,* as the true starting point of Steinbeck's career as a significant writer, to show us where he was coming from and what he had to say about it. The story-cycles, however, have never received their due and need innovative promotion, while Steinbeck's second and last big novel (which Bloom rejects out of hand) is uniquely important for autobiographical reasons to such a cult as Steinbeck has developed, even if it, like *Gone With the Wind,* belongs to a genre that is not usually considered "classic" academically.

Still, the matter most needing scrutiny remains the widespread emphasis on Steinbeck's three novels of the late 1930s about migrant agricultural laborers as the peak of his achievement, for it touches on recently hotly debated questions about the canon of American fiction generally.

Bloom raises this issue in a most cogent form when he observes, "Whether a human strength, however generously worked through, is also an aesthetic value, in a literary narrative, is one of those larger issues that literary criticism scarcely knows how to decide" (5). The last clause of this statement is somewhat fuzzy, with "literary criticism" treated as a self-determining consciousness, but Bloom fudges about the avoidance of "the larger issue" involved because it is one that modern criticism has been reluctant to confront. The "human strength" dealt with in Steinbeck's novels is *survival*. What flourished as criticism through the first studies of American literature employed the prevailing circular reasoning that Joyce satirized in *A Portrait of the Artist as a Young Man*: that a good work of literature was the work of a good writer, defined as one who produced works that respectable society approved.[1] Survival was viewed not as an individual right but as a social value, and one's fate was determined by compliance with canons of respectability. Melville's shocking allegories, for example, were shunned for challenging accepted norms.

As "Victorian compromises" failed and canons of respectability came under fire, this school gave way in the grim 1930s to a then New Criticism, which shifted attention from the personality of the artist to the autonomous work of art and cultivated an ironic attitude toward the vanity of human wishes that questioned the very emphasis on survival itself. (The complicated sensibility behind a key poem like Allen Tate's "Ode to the Confederate Dead" cannot be treated at length here, but it needs to be suggested as a basis for understanding the opposition of elitist critics to writers like Steinbeck. Basically, to use terms from Steinbeck's *Cup of Gold* employed throughout this study, it accepts "going under" rather than splitting before a "civilization" that one might describe, as Ezra Pound does in "Hugh Selwyn Mauberley," as "an old bitch gone in the teeth.")

Since Steinbeck's death, authoritarian modes of criticism have replaced the New Criticism that some rejected as overly histrionic in favor of postulating a position that nothing really means anything. Finding the struggle to escape societal bonds futile, one puts up with some arbitrary "word" as a means of imposing order on fundamental chaos (particular "words" are promoted by manipulative techniques by those who will profit most from the projected "order"). "Survival" thus becomes a matter of self-seeking gains rather than self-transcendence— something that Steinbeck seems to have sensed but could not, with failing powers, find an artistic form to project as he had the achievement of self-transcendence over the previously accepted norms of bourgeois pieties in *The Grapes of Wrath* and *Cannery Row*. Bloom is an articulate spokesman for an immediate postwar position that rejects subsequent "minimalism" because of its narcissism, but he squirms about breaking with traditional canons of respectability because he shares some of Steinbeck's own problems about the works climaxing in self-transcendence, though not for the same reasons.

Bloom comments—again speaking for many others—that one thing that remains in Steinbeck's work is its "fairly constant popularity with an immense number of liberal middlebrows, both in his own country and abroad," leaving an impression that his was what Steinbeck defiantly sought to cultivate. But Steinbeck, in attacking the vigilante mentality controlling his native postfrontier rural society, was *not* writing for liberal middlebrows. He sought rather, with the same naïveté that was the undoing of fanatical "proletarian writers" with whom the insensitive opposition confused him, to write works that he thought would not be popular with the usual book-buying public, addressed to the people he was writing about, trying to provide an artistic example that would inspire self-confidence. Like others so motivated, he found it impossible to make this breakthrough, but in the process he was able to attract—with greater success than others—the liberal middlebrows.

The Grapes of Wrath was thus, from the writer's viewpoint, in one sense a magnificent failure, for while it produced unanticipated large returns, these also produced unanticipated troubles, while at the same time it reached and influenced not its intended audience but instead the earnest, "realistic" one he had always scorned. He was writing survival literature in the tradition of Stephen Crane's *The Red Badge of Courage* and Joseph Conrad's *Heart of Darkness* and *The Secret Sharer* which presented survival as an aesthetic value through the detailed portrayal of a creative individual who shapes from the raw material of self an object of art to transcend the encompassing chaos. Elitists shuddered, however, at the prospect of a self-realized Jim Nolan or Tom Joad—or even Doc—among the riffraff.

Placing Jim Nolan from *In Dubious Battle* with Tom Joad and Doc raises, since Jim meets a faceless death, the question of whether this novel and *Of Mice and Men* are also survival novels. (George does survive but, his dream destroyed, becomes a precursor of the figures in postmodernist fiction that Steinbeck rejected with *The Grapes of Wrath*.)

They are not, in the sense that they should be optimistic about the present situation, but neither is *The Grapes of Wrath*, which does not fatuously suppose the underlying problems solved but offers only a possibility of hope if people begin to understand the situation and take unfashionable action to solve it. In a subtle way, however, they refute most of Bloom's comments about them while justifying his placement of them.

In his first major works, *The Pastures of Heaven* and *The Red Pony*, Steinbeck, already mounting his attack on respectable middle-class inhibitions, was deadly ironic in the alienated modernist vein and saw coming to terms with reality as only a depressing but maturing experience. Their value is that they do establish, as clearly as the early works of Fitzgerald and Hemingway, the position from which he was to move.

Tortilla Flat was indeed, as Steinbeck acknowledged, "second-rate," because among other reasons cited earlier, despite Steinbeck's affection for his characters, readers were not taking it seriously in the sense that they cared whether Danny self-destructed and his company was scattered. It provided escapist entertainment at a time when the country needed it—the *paisanos* were amusingly shocking but one would not want them around the house. They were no more disturbing than W. C. Fields's outrageous antics in the movies.

To *In Dubious Battle* and *Of Mice and Men,* however, Steinbeck added a new ingredient. Jim Nolan was destroyed and George turned into a kind of zombie, because Steinbeck wanted readers to be outraged by what had happened. And what readers can still experience after these fictional encounters is outrage toward the terrible waste of the caring and capable that is the result of insensible human violence. They are angry novels that prompt not acquiescence in the inevitability of what has happened but defiance toward the thwarting of survival—the same spirit that informs Hemingway's *To Have and Have Not* and Faulkner's monumental *Absalom, Absalom!*

There is outrage also, of course, in *The Grapes of Wrath,* but the author here wishes to leave readers with an enticing possibility of hope, as Joseph Heller does in *Catch-22.* The earlier novels are preliminary, but they are more than period pieces; they are warnings about what happens when things are placed above people or people are used as things. The line between sentimentality and compassion escapes clear distinction, but if compassion is not an aesthetic value, art petrifies, so that one must discriminate carefully in this area.

What Bloom does not deal with at all is *Cannery Row.* Has he even considered a work usually casually dismissed? It was certainly not aimed at the liberal middlebrow audience. Its caustic irony in invocatory statements like "What can it profit a man to gain the whole world and to come to his property with a gastric ulcer, a blown prostate and bifocals?" is directed specifically at this group that had taken with such seriousness Steinbeck's grimly ironic novels.

The test here is a severe one for the readers, because the cognoscenti might easily scoff at such pathetic strainings toward the beautiful. Steinbeck's point, however, at the time he was in the transient mood in which he was driven to write this novel, was that the unique human quality was the recollection of aesthetic experiences. One need not rush to war-ravaged Europe, where the classic paintings were in bomb shelters anyway, nor have a season ticket to Toscanini's concerts to consecrate oneself to the celebration of Pater's "gemlike flame" that art kept alight in a world where "ignorant armies clash by night." It is not immediate sensory experience but the spirit of one's involvement that matters. A clod's nature is not changed by saturation exposure to art treasures, as Orson Welles's *Citizen Kane* manifests, and a devotee may live through periods of bleak exile on memories alone. Even if Steinbeck could not sustain the vision embodied in his novel, he had this one time embodied a human strength of survival's depending not just on an indomitable will but on a self-effacement before the race's finest achievements that makes survival worthwhile.

One may genuinely regret that in his later years Steinbeck—like many others who had earlier made creative contributions to American culture—did not publicly recognize his kinship with the beat generation. But he was probably put off, like so many, by those who had been sensationalized by the press as beatniks. He gave no indication that he recognized how close to his own imprecations in *Cannery Row* were such key sentiments in Allen Ginsberg's *Howl* as his description of "the three old shrews of fate the one eyed shrew of the heterosexual dollar the one eyed shrew that winks out of the womb and the one eyed shrew that does nothing but sit on her ass and snip the intellectual golden threads of the craftsman's loom"[2]—the classical Fates restored by a consumerist culture.

When Steinbeck's publisher began a brief association with Jack Kerouac, Steinbeck wrote to Chase Horton (who would edit his Malory adaptations) shortly after *On the Road* was published, "I have more respect for the craft than I ever had, much more because I know its hugeness and to some extent my own limitations. The angry young men and the Beats are simply trying to add velocity to the other three dimensions as they should. . . . It requires a language which has not been made yet but the Beats are working on it and they may create it."[3] The beats never did, except in fragments, sidetracked by the same forces that plunged Steinbeck back into active participation in the ill-fated course of American middlebrow liberals' do-gooding during the crises of the Kennedy and Johnson administrations.

Doc of *Cannery Row,* whose "mind had no horizon and his sympathy . . . no warp," is on the same frequency as the beat movement as its essence was conveyed by Allen Ginsberg:

I think there was one slight shade of error in describing the Beat movement as primarily a protest movement, particularly Abbie [Hoffman].
That was the thing that Kerouac was always complaining about; he felt
the literary aspect or the spiritual aspect or the emotional aspect was not
so much protest at all but a declaration of unconditioned mind beyond
protest, beyond resentment, beyond loser, beyond *winner*—*way* beyond
winner—beyond winner or loser, a declaration of *unconditioned mind,* a
visionary declaration, a declaration of *unworldly love* that has *no hope* of the
world and cannot change the world to its desire. . . . [T]he basic theme
was beyond the rights and wrongs of political protest.[4]

The sentiment of having no hope of changing the world to one's
desire is surely too unworldly for Steinbeck's work after *Cannery Row,* but
the statements about going beyond political protest certainly fit his
intentions for his best work from *The Pastures of Heaven* to *Cannery Row.*
One cannot predict what Steinbeck's reputation will be in another century, but one can hope that these links will be recognized in forming it.
The world was at times too much with him, but at his best moments, as
with the Beauties, Virtues, and Graces of *Cannery Row,* he avoided its
traps.

Notes and References

Preface

1. Warren French, "Steinbeck and Modernism," in *Steinbeck's Prophetic Vision of America,* ed. Tetsumaro Hayashi and Kenneth D. Swan (Upland, Ind.: Taylor University, 1976), 35–55; repr. in *Critical Essays on Steinbeck's "The Grapes of Wrath,"* ed. John Ditsky (Boston: G. K. Hall, 1989), 152–62.

2. Harold Bloom, ed., *Modern Critical Views: John Steinbeck* (New York: Chelsea House, 1987), 1; hereafter cited in text as Bloom.

Chapter One

1. This chapter title plays upon the title of Harry Geduld and Ron Gottesman's *Sergei Eisenstein and Upton Sinclair: The Making and Unmaking of "Que Viva Mexico!"* (Bloomington: Indiana University Press, 1970), another chronicle of a sensitive social consciousness caught in California's long battle between idealism and commercialism.

2. Elaine Steinbeck and Robert Wallsten, eds., *Steinbeck: A Life in Letters* (New York: Viking, 1975), 108; hereafter cited in text as *Life*.

3. Jackson J. Benson, *The True Adventures of John Steinbeck, Writer* (New York: Viking, 1984), 27; hereafter cited in text as Benson. Biographical information not specifically quoted has been checked against this book.

4. Robert DeMott, *Steinbeck's Reading* (New York: Garland, 1984), locates several of William Blake's books in Steinbeck's library as early as 1933 but quotes him as remarking to Bennett Cerf of Random House in 1938, "How little of Blake I have really read"; hereafter cited in text as *Reading*.

5. Lewis Gannett, preface to *Cup of Gold* (New York: Covici, Friede, 1936), v.

6. During the 1930s Steinbeck displayed a phenomenal ability to reproduce lost texts. After he finished the first "Red Pony" story, he misplaced the manuscript. When it turned up three years later, only seven words differed in the reproduced version (Benson, 330).

7. See Warren French, "The First Theatrical Performance of *Of Mice and Men,*" *American Literature* 36 (January 1965): 525–27.

8. *Working Days: The Journal of "The Grapes of Wrath,"* ed. Robert DeMott (New York: Viking, 1989), xxxvi; hereafter cited in text as *Working Days*.

9. See Warren French, ed., *A Companion to "The Grapes of Wrath"* (New York: Viking, 1963), 93–101; for later, detailed accounts of the migrants' influence in California, see Gerald Haslam, *Coming of Age in California* (Walnut

Creek, Calif.: Devil Mountain Books, 1990), and *The Other California: The Great Central Valley in Life and Letters* (Santa Barbara, Calif.: Capra Press, 1990), as well as James N. Gregory, *American Exodus: The Dust Bowl and Okie Culture in California* (New York: Oxford University Press, 1989).

   10. See Roy S. Simmonds, "The Original Manuscript," *San Jose Studies* 16 (Winter 1990), 117–132, for a detailed comparison of the holograph with the published text. Simmonds comments that, with few exceptions, everything remains the same from the opening to the closing sentences. He ends with the comment that Steinbeck had been "burned out by his prodigious efforts" (129).

   11. See Richard Astro, *John Steinbeck and Edward F. Ricketts: The Shaping of a Novelist* (Minneapolis: University of Minnesota Press, 1973), 57–60, for details of the disagreement that prompted Ricketts to write, "Thesis and Materials for a Script on Mexico," which he considered as an "anti-script" to Steinbeck's; hereafter cited as Astro, *JS & R,* in text.

   12. Robert DeMott gave the poems a collective title when he presented them with commentary in his "After *The Grapes of Wrath:* A Speculative Essay on John Steinbeck's Suite of Love Poems for Gwyn, 'The Girl in the Air,' " in *John Steinbeck: The Years of Greatness, 1936–1939,* ed. Tetsumaro Hayashi (Tuscaloosa: University of Alabama Press, 1993), 20–45.

   13. Joseph E. Millichap, *Steinbeck and Film* (New York: Ungar, 1983), 74; hereafter cited in text.

   14. *The Wayward Bus* (New York: Viking, 1947), 3; hereafter cited in the text as *Bus.* Steinbeck was nearing 50 when he wrote the novel.

   15. Thomas H. Pauly, *An American Odyssey: Elia Kazan and American Culture* (Philadelphia: Temple University Press, 1983), 146–49.

   16. Thomas Fensch, *Steinbeck and Covici: The Story of a Friendship* (Middlebury, Vt.: Paul S. Eriksson, 1979), 115; hereafter cited in text as Fensch.

   17. *Burning Bright* (New York: Viking, 1950), 108; hereafter cited in text as *Burning.*

   18. "Critics, Critics, Burning Bright," *Saturday Review,* 27 August 1955, 20.

   19. Roy S. Simmonds, "John [Ernst] Steinbeck," *Twentieth Century Romance and Historical Writers,* 2nd ed. (Chicago and London: St. James Press, 1990), 613.

Chapter Two

   1. Roy S. Simmonds, *Steinbeck's Literary Achievement,* Steinbeck Monograph Series, no. 6 (Muncie, Ind.: The John Steinbeck Society of America, 1976), 28; hereafter cited in text as *Achievement.*

   2. Wayne C. Booth, *The Rhetoric of Fiction* (Chicago: University of Chicago Press, 1961), 7.

   3. "How Mr. Hogan Robbed a Bank," in *The Portable Steinbeck,* rev. ed., ed. Pascal Covici, Jr. (New York: Viking, 1971), 639.

4. Jacques Barzun, *Classic, Romantic, and Modern* (Garden City, N.Y.: Doubleday Anchor Books, 1961), 115.

5. Burnshaw's symposium also includes an essay by Harry Levin asking specifically "What Was Modernism?," but it was less concerned with defining this sensibility than with nostalgically reminiscing about its principal practitioners.

6. Lionel Trilling, "The Modern Element in Literature," in *Varieties of Literary Experience*, ed. Stanley Burnshaw (New York: New York University Press, 1962), 433.

7. Maurice Beebe, "What Modernism Was," *Journal of Modern Literature* 3 (July 1974): 1065–84.

8. Quoted in Marston LaFrance, *A Reading of Stephen Crane* (Oxford: Clarendon Press, 1971), 3, translated from David F. Swann and Walter Lourie, *Concluding Unscientific Postscript* (Princeton, N.J.: Princeton University Press, 1941), 448–50.

Chapter Three

1. *Cup of Gold* (New York: Covici, Friede, 1936), 254–55; hereafter cited in text as *Cup.*

2. Steinbeck at last makes the escapist artist the central figure in *Cannery Row* (see chapter 9).

3. Richard Astro, "Phlebas Sails the Caribbean: Steinbeck, Hemingway, and the American Waste Land," in *The Twenties: Fiction Poetry, Drama* (Deland, Fl.: Everett/Edwards, 1975), 221.

4. *To a God Unknown* (New York: Bantam Books, 1955), 145–46.

5. *The Grapes of Wrath* (New York: Viking, 1939).

Chapter Four

1. Forrest L. Ingram, *Representative Short-Story Cycles of the Twentieth Century* (The Hague: Mouton, 1971), 15.

2. The complete text of this important letter to Steinbeck's agent Mavis McIntosh, dated 8 May 1931, from Pacific Grove, California, is in *Life*, 42–43. Steinbeck also explains that he changed the name of Corral de Tierra (Earthly Garden) and that of the Morans to Munroe "because I am using its people."

3. *The Pastures of Heaven* (New York: Covici, Friede, 1936), 294; hereafter cited in text as *Pastures.*

4. Joseph Fontenrose, *Steinbeck's Unhappy Valley* (Berkeley, Calif., 1981), 46–47.

5. Louis Owens, *John Steinbeck's Re-vision of America* (Athens: University of Georgia Press, 1985), 89; hereafter cited in text as *Re-vision.*

6. *The Red Pony* (New York: Viking, 1945), 13. Subsequent page references are to this edition, illustrated by Wesley Dennis, as it is the first commercial publication of the four stories collected as a cycle.

7. For further discussion of the mythical quality of the narrative, see Warren French, "John Steinbeck and American Literature," *San Jose Studies* 13 (Spring 1987): 41–43, which discusses *The Red Pony* as depicting "a regional rite of passage" as explained in Northrop Frye's analysis of "the seasonal cycle of the year" in "The Archetypes of Literature," *Kenyon Review* 13 (1951): 104–105.

8. Steinbeck's "Narration" and correspondence relating to it are in the Annie Laurie Williams Collection in the Rare Book and Manuscript Library, Butler Library, Columbia University, New York. Williams handled permissions for Steinbeck's agents.

9. For a detailed comparison of the film with the story-cycle, see Warren French, "*The Red Pony* as Story Cycle and Film," in *The Short Novels of John Steinbeck,* ed. Jackson J. Benson (Durham, N.C.: Duke University Press, 1990), 71–94.

10. Millichap in *Steinbeck and Film* attributes Steinbeck's transformation of "his realistic initiation tale into a sentimental imitation of initiation" (177) to "the artistic climate of the Hollywood studio system" (109), but director Lewis Milestone and Steinbeck had a freer hand than usual with their independent production; the changes are closely related to Steinbeck's tendency toward upbeat moralizing and writing with his sons in mind after World War II.

11. Frank Norris, *The Octopus* (1901; reprint, Garden City, NY: Doubleday, Doran, 1928), 2:214.

Chapter Five

1. Criticism of the stories discussed in this chapter has been particularly influenced by the gathering of the work of a new generation of critics in *Steinbeck's Short Stories in "The Long Valley": Essays in Criticism,* Steinbeck Monograph Series, No. 15 (Muncie, Ind.: Steinbeck Research Institute, 1991); hereafter cited in text as *Stories.*

2. Edwin H. Cady, *The Light of Common Day: Realism in American Fiction* (Bloomington: Indiana University Press, 1971), 51, 47.

3. *The Long Valley* (New York: Covici, Friede, 1938), 29; hereafter cited in text as *LV.*

4. The problems posed by the variant texts of "The Chrysanthemums" are discussed in Roy S. Simmonds, "The Original Manuscripts of Steinbeck's 'The Chrysanthemums,' " *Steinbeck Quarterly* 7 (Summer–Fall 1974): 102–11. Steinbeck apparently established the final text for the collection when reviewing it for publication in 1938. Simmonds stresses the sexually charged aspects of the story and argues provocatively that "the tinker had, by that one action of throwing the flowers away, symbolically re-established the position of male dominance she imagined she had wrested from him, in exactly the same way as over the years she had deprived, emasculated her husband." He does not consider the problems posed by the tinker's being described as a "bargainer" in the *Harper's* text. Steinbeck may not have authorized this editorial change, but the tinker's preference for the pot over the flowers also puts him among those

tradespeople whom Steinbeck detested for lacking an intimate relation to nature such as Elisa has.

5. Patricia M. Mandia, "Sexism and Racism, or Irony? Steinbeck's 'The Murder,' " in *Stories,* 69.

Chapter Six

1. See David G. Pugh, "Reading the Proletarians—Thirty Years Later," in *The Thirties: Fiction, Poetry, Drama,* ed. Warren French (Deland, Fla.: Everett/Edwards, 1967), 89–95, for a discussion of finding it "difficult to maintain that willing suspension of disbelief which constitutes poetic faith," reading in 1965 the selections in Granville Hicks, ed., *Proletarian Literature in the United States* (New York: International Publishers, 1935).

2. The twilight city in which the action begins resembles Carol Steinbeck's hometown of San Jose, California, where the Communist party maintained its regional headquarters for organizing migrant laborers. But neither the city nor the party is identified, because Steinbeck wished to universalize, not particularize, the situation.

3. *Of Mice and Men* (New York: Covici, Friede, 1937), 129–30.

Chapter Seven

1. *The Grapes of Wrath* (New York: Viking Press, 1939), 32–33; hereafter cited in text.

2. Frederic I. Carpenter, "The Philosophical Joads," *College English* 2 (January 1941): 315–25.

3. *The Log from the Sea of Cortez* (New York: Viking, 1962), 150; hereafter cited in text as *Log.*

4. Clifton Fadiman, "Books," *New Yorker,* 15 April 1939, 81.

5. Lionel Trilling, "Artists and the 'Societal Function,' " *Speaking of Literature and Society* (New York: Harcourt Brace Jovanovich, 1980), 189; repr. from *Kenyon Review,* 1942.

6. Peter Lisca, *The Wide World of John Steinbeck* (New Brunswick, N.J.: Rutgers University Press, 1958), 167–68; hereafter cited in text as Lisca.

7. *The Forgotten Village* (New York; Viking, 1942), preface, unpaged.

8. Translation follows C. H. Grandgent, *Dante* (New York: Duffield, 1916), 273–75; for a full discussion of the application of Dante's theories to *The Grapes of Wrath,* see Tetsumaro Hayashi, ed., *A Study Guide to Steinbeck* (Metuchen, N.J.: Scarecrow, 1974), 35–41.

7. Grandgent, *Dante,* 275.

Chapter Eight

1. *The Moon Is Down* (New York: Viking, 1942), 143.

2. *Bombs Away: The Story of a Bomber Team* (New York: Viking, 1942), 13–14.

3. See Millichap, 76–85, for a discussion of the differences between Steinbeck's story treatment and Hitchcock's film, as well as Steinbeck's disgusted reaction to the film and its director.

Chapter Nine

1. *Cannery Row* (New York: Viking, 1945), 10; hereafter cited in text as *Row.*

Chapter Ten

1. Jack Kerouac, *On the Road* (New York: Viking, 1957), 148.
2. Lawrence William Jones, *John Steinbeck as Fabulist,* Steinbeck Monograph Series, no. 3 (Muncie, Ind.: The John Steinbeck Society of America, 1973), 23; hereafter cited in text as Jones.
3. Robert E. Morsberger, "Steinbeck's Zapata: Rebel versus Revolutionary," in *Viva Zapata!* (New York: Viking, 1975), xxvi.
4. See Warren French, "Fiction vs. Film, 1960–1985," in *Contemporary American Fiction,* ed. Malcolm Bradbury and Sigmund Ro (London: Edward Arnold, 1987), 106–21, for a discussion of the differences between fiction as an evocative medium and film as a concrete one.

Chapter Eleven

1. Howard Levant, *The Novels of John Steinbeck* (Columbia: University of Missouri Press, 1974), 234; hereafter cited in text as Levant.
2. Joseph Fontenrose, *John Steinbeck: An Introduction and Interpretation* (New York: Barnes & Noble, 1963), 126–27.
3. F. W. Watt, *Steinbeck* (Edinburgh: Oliver & Boyd, 1962), 93.
4. Lester J. Marks, *"East of Eden:* 'Thou Mayest,' " *Steinbeck Quarterly* 4 (Winter 1971): 18.
5. Pascal Covici, Jr., "From Commitment to Choice: Double Vision and the Problem of Vitality for John Steinbeck," in *The Fifties: Fiction, Drama, Poetry,* ed. Warren French (Deland, Fla.: Everett/Edwards, 1970), 65, 71.
6. Warren French, *John Steinbeck,* 2nd ed. rev. (Boston: Twayne, 1975), 152.
7. Paul McCarthy, *John Steinbeck* (New York: Ungar, 1980), 123.
8. Daniel Buerger, " 'History' and Fiction in *East of Eden* Criticism," *Steinbeck Quarterly* 14 (Winter–Spring 1981): 13.
9. See Millichap, 168–70.
10. See Erwin Panofsky, *"Et in Arcadia Ego:* Poussin and the Elegiac Tradition," in *Meaning in the Visual Arts* (Garden City, N.Y.: Doubleday, 1955), 295–320, for a discussion of the Arcadian symbol in the pastoral.

Chapter Twelve

1. *The Short Reign of Pippin IV* (New York: Viking, 1957), 139.
2. *The Winter of Our Discontent* (New York: Viking, 1961), 294.
3. Ken Kesey, *One Flew over the Cuckoo's Nest* (New York: Viking, 1962), 203–04.
4. *America and Americans* (New York: Viking, 1966), 127–28.

Chapter Thirteen

1. See Gene Ruoff, "The New Criticism: One Child of the 30s That Grew Up," in *The Thirties: Fiction, Poetry, Drama,* ed. Warren French (Deland, Fla.: Everett/Edwards, 1967), 169–74, for a comparison of New Critical techniques with those of the previously predominating academic criticism.
2. Allen Ginsberg, *Howl: Original Draft Facsimile, Transcript, and Variant Versions,* ed. Barry Miles (New York: Harper & Row, 1986), 4.
3. *King Arthur and His Noble Knights* (New York: Farrar, Straus & Giroux, 1976), 326.
4. Quoted in Paul Krassner, "High Noon at Camp Kerouac," *The Beat Road (Unspeakable Visions of the Individual)* (California, Pa.: Arthur & Kit Knight, 1984), 14:11.

Selected Bibliography

PRIMARY WORKS
Novels

Bombs Away: The Story of a Bomber Team. New York: Viking Press, 1942.
Burning Bright. New York: Viking Press, 1950.
Cannery Row. New York: Viking Press, 1945.
Cup of Gold. New York: Robert M. McBride, 1929; reissued, New York: Covici, Friede, 1936.
In Dubious Battle. New York: Covici, Friede, 1936.
East of Eden. New York: Viking Press, 1952.
The Grapes of Wrath. New York: Viking Press, 1939; with lithographs by Thomas Hart Benton (New York: Limited Editions Club, 1940); Fiftieth-Anniversary edition, with introduction by Studs Terkel, 1989.
Of Mice and Men. New York: Covici, Friede, 1937.
The Moon Is Down. New York: Viking Press, 1942.
The Pastures of Heaven. New York: Brewer, Warren & Putnam, 1932.
The Pearl. New York: Viking Press, 1947.
The Short Reign of Pippin IV. New York: Viking Press, 1957.
Sweet Thursday. New York: Viking Press, 1954.
To a God Unknown. New York: Robert O. Ballou, 1933.
Tortilla Flat. New York: Covici, Friede, 1935.
The Wayward Bus. New York: Viking Press, 1947.
The Winter of Our Discontent. New York: Viking Press, 1961.

Short Stories

The Long Valley. New York: Viking Press, 1938. Includes "The Chrysanthemums," "The White Quail," "Flight," "The Snake," "Breakfast," "The Raid," "The Harness," "The Vigilante," "Johnny Bear," "The Murder," "St. Katy the Virgin," and *The Red Pony.*
Nothing So Monstrous. New York: Covici, Friede, 1936. Separate printing of chapter 6 of *The Pastures of Heaven,* with additional material by the author as a limited-edition Christmas greeting.
The Red Pony. New York: Covici, Friede, 1937. A limited-edition including "The Gift," "The Great Mountains," and "The Promise"; with illustrations by Wesley Dennis (New York: Viking Press, 1945), including "The Leader of the People."
Saint Katy the Virgin. New York: Covici, Friede, 1936. Limited edition of 199 copies signed by author.

Filmscripts

The Forgotten Village. New York: Viking Press, 1941. Text of voice-over narration, with a preface by the author and 136 stills from the film.

Viva Zapata! Edited with an introduction, "Steinbeck's Zapata: Rebel versus Revolutionary," by Robert Morsberger. New York: Viking Press, 1975; without Morsberger's introduction and with annotations in Japanese by Kiyohiko Tsuboi and Kyoko Ariki (Tokyo: The Eihosha, 1985).

Zapata, ed. Robert Morsberger. New York: Penguin, 1992. First publication of the prose narrative about Mexican President Emiliano Zapata, on which the film *Viva Zapata!* was based, along with Steinbeck's screenplay and notes on the film production by director Elia Kazan.

Plays

Burning Bright (acting edition only). New York: Dramatists Play Service, 1951.
Of Mice and Men. New York: Covici, Friede, 1937.
The Moon Is Down. New York: Viking Press, 1943.

Modernization

The Acts of King Arthur and His Noble Knights. New York: Farrar, Straus & Giroux, 1976. There is no accepted term that precisely describes this unique work. It is described on the title page as "From the Winchester Mss. of Thomas Malory and Other Sources, edited by Horton Chase." Steinbeck did not complete or edit the work, but in a prefatory note he writes, "For a long time I have wanted to bring to present-day usage the stories of King Arthur and the Knights of the Round Table." Excerpts from letters written between 1956 and 1965 in which Steinbeck discusses the project are appended.

Autobiography

Steinbeck never published a formal autobiography, but a number of his publications are accounts of his life and thoughts, particularly at the time of the writing, so that an account of many of his most important activities can be pieced together.

America and Americans. New York: Viking 1966. "A book of opinions, unashamed and individual," highlighted by many personal reminiscences and accompanied by 136 pages of black-and-white and color photographs of scenes typical of American life.

Un Américaine à New York et à Paris. Paris: René Julliard, 1956. A collection of short articles that Steinbeck wrote in English for the daily newspaper *Le Figaro* during his residence in Paris in 1954, translated into French by

Jean-François Rozan. Some short fictional pieces are included. The collection has not been published in English.

Journal of a Novel: The "East of Eden" Letters. New York: Viking, 1969. Letters addressed to the editor, Pascal Covici, during the writing of the novel, discussing its progress.

Once There Was a War. New York: Viking Press, 1958. Dispatches written from London and the Mediterranean war zone in 1943, with a new introduction by the author.

Positano. Salerno, Italy: Ente Provinciale per il Turismo, 1954. A paean of praise for the colorful Italian coastal resort on a hillside. Originally a May 1953 article for *Harper's Bazaar;* the Italian tourist board has reprinted it in several languages.

A Russian Journal. New York: Viking Press, 1948. An account of a trip to Russia in 1947, illustrated with photographs by Robert Capa.

Sea of Cortez, with Edward F. Ricketts. New York: Viking Press, 1941. Record of an expedition to study the marine life of the Gulf of California littoral, with many color plates of specimens. *The Log* (text) alone was subsequently published separately, with an essay, "About Ed Ricketts" (New York: Viking Press, 1951).

Speech Accepting the Nobel Prize for Literature. New York: Viking Press, 1962. Limited edition of 3,200 copies; not for sale.

Their Blood Is Strong. San Francisco: Simon J. Lubin Society of California, 1938. Reports to the *San Francisco News* of conditions in the migrant camps in 1936 and the author's recommendation about handling the tragedy, with an updated conclusion.

Travels with Charley in Search of America. New York: Viking Press, 1962. An account of the author's transcontinental tour with a giant poodle to get reacquainted with his country.

Working Days: The Journals of "The Grapes of Wrath." 1938–41. Edited by Robert DeMott. New York: Viking Press, 1989. Transcription of a daily journal kept by Steinbeck while writing the novel between May and October 1938, with additional diary entries and an introduction and notes by the editor.

Anthologies

The Portable Steinbeck. Selected by Pascal Covici. New York: Viking Press, 1943; revised edition, with an introduction by Lewis Gannett (New York: Viking Press, 1946); revised, selected, and introduced by Pascal Covici, Jr. (New York: Viking Press, 1974).

The Short Novels of John Steinbeck. With an introduction by Joseph Henry Jackson. New York: Viking Press, 1953. Contains *Cannery Row, The Moon Is Down, Of Mice and Men, The Pearl, The Red Pony, and Tortilla Flat.*

The Steinbeck Pocket Book. Selected by Pascal Covici. New York: The Blakiston
Company–Pocket Books, 1943.

SECONDARY WORKS

Bibliography

DeMott, Robert. *John Steinbeck: A Checklist of Books by and About.* Bradenton,
Fla.: Opuscula, 1987.
French, Warren. "John Steinbeck." In *Sixteen Modern American Authors.*
Durham, N.C.: Duke University Press, vol. 1, 1974, 499–527; vol. 2,
1989, 582–622.
Hayashi, Tetsumaro. *A New Steinbeck Bibliography, 1929–1971.* Metuchen, N.J.:
Scarecrow Press, 1973; *Supplement I, 1971–1981,* 1983.
Nakayama, Kiyoshi. *Steinbeck in Japan: A Bibliography, 1939–1992.* Osaka:
Kansai University Press, 1992.

Dictionary

Hayashi, Tetsumaro, ed. *John Steinbeck: A Dictionary of His Fictional Characters.*
Metuchen, N.J.: Scarecrow Press, 1976. An alphabetical listing of characters in Steinbeck's fiction with discussions of their roles.

Biography

A number of short biographies designed to interest young people and casual
readers add little to the record provided by the books listed. An authorized biography by Jay Parini has been announced by Heinemann
(London) for 1994 publication. Roy Simmonds's account of the critical
years of World War II is also in preparation.
Benson, Jackson J. *The True Adventures of John Steinbeck, Writer.* New York:
Viking Press, 1984. The more than 1,000-page result of Benson's 13-
year quest for information for this first detailed biography that marks the
beginning of a new era in the understanding and criticism of this author
who shunned publicity. An interesting by-product of this monumental
labor was Benson's *Looking for Steinbeck's Ghost* (Norman: University of
Oklahoma Press, 1988), his account of his long search, which contains
additional material about Steinbeck. For an account of Benson and his
work, see my entry in *American Literary Biographers, Dictionary of Literary
Biography* 111 (Detroit: Gale Research, 1991), 16–24.
DeMott, Robert J. *Steinbeck's Reading.* New York: Garland, 1984. A list of nearly 1,000 books that Steinbeck is known to have owned or borrowed,
annotated with many of his comments about them and many notes by
DeMott that provide much biographical information about the novelist.
Two supplements by DeMott have appeared in *Steinbeck Quarterly* 17
(Summer–Fall 1984): 97–103 and 22 (Winter–Spring 1989): 4–8.

Enea, Sparky, as told to Audry Lynch. *With Steinbeck in the Sea of Cortez.* Los Osos, Calif.: Sand River Press, 1991. A gossipy, illustrated account by the cook on the *Western Flyer,* supplementing the Steinbeck-Ricketts "Log" of the 1940 expedition into the Gulf of California.

Fensch, Thomas. *Steinbeck and Covici: The Story of a Friendship.* Middlebury, Vt.: Paul S. Erikkson, 1979. Valuable for its extensive record of full texts from Steinbeck's long correspondence with Pascal Covici, who was his publisher and editor from 1935 until the novelist's death; the commentary, however, is limited to minimal annotations.

Hayashi, Tetsumaro. *John Steinbeck and the Vietnam War.* Part 1. Muncie, Ind.: The Steinbeck Research Institute, 1986. Presents from a sympathetic viewpoint Steinbeck's growing pessimism about the conflict he came to regard as a personal and national tragedy. No further parts have been published.

————. *John Steinbeck on Writing.* Muncie, Ind.: The Steinbeck Research Institute, 1988. A rewarding scrapbook of quotations from Steinbeck's publications and letters, followed by a brief essay, "John Steinbeck: The Art and Craft of Writing."

Sheffield, Carlton A. *Steinbeck: The Good Companion.* Portola Valley, Calif.: American Lives Endowment, 1983. An invaluable account by "Dook," one of Steinbeck's close friends at Stanford; unfortunately, it is poorly published as photocopies from corrected, typed sheets.

Steinbeck, Elaine, and Robert Wallsten, eds. *Steinbeck: A Life in Letters.* New York: Viking Press, 1975. The first posthumous biography of the author that uses entire and excerpted letters incorporated into a running chronological account by Steinbeck's widow and a close friend to outline the story of his life.

Criticism: General Estimates

Only monographs and symposia are listed. Consult the bibliographies listed earlier for articles and essays.

Astro, Richard. *John Steinbeck and Edward F. Ricketts: The Shaping of a Novelist.* Minneapolis: University of Minnesota Press, 1973. An analysis of the influence of the marine biologist on Steinbeck's career that should be checked against Benson's biography.

————, and Tetsumaro Hayashi, eds. *Steinbeck: The Man and His Work.* Corvallis: Oregon State University Press, 1971. Collects 10 biographical and critical articles on Steinbeck's novels and filmscripts, delivered at a conference in 1970.

————, and Joel W. Hedgpeth. *Steinbeck and the Sea.* Corvallis: Oregon State University, Sea Grant College Program, 1975. Presents the proceedings of a conference held at the Marine Science Center Auditorium, Newport, Oregon, 4 May 1974.

Benson, Jackson J., ed. *The Short Novels of John Steinbeck.* Durham, N.C.: Duke University Press, 1990. A collection of 13 previously unpublished essays and 10 reprints of articles by major Steinbeck scholars on nine short novels. Includes Steinbeck's introduction to the collection of six novels published in 1953 and a comprehensive checklist of criticism.

Bloom, Harold, ed. *John Steinbeck.* Modern Critical Views. New York: Chelsea House, 1987. Part of an extensive program of critiques of important modern works, edited and introduced by the Yale critic, collecting 11 essays published between 1947 and 1985.

Davis, Robert Murray, ed. *Steinbeck: A Collection of Critical Essays.* Twentieth Century Views Series. Englewood Cliffs, N.J.: Prentice Hall, 1972. Reprints a dozen essays by some of the best-known Steinbeck scholars as part of an extensive series edited by Maynard Mack.

Fontenrose, Joseph. *John Steinbeck: An Introduction and an Interpretation.* New York: Barnes & Noble, 1963. A distinguished California classical scholar and friend of Steinbeck's family provides a pioneering account of the variety of mythological materials influencing Steinbeck's fiction.

French, Warren. *John Steinbeck.* New York: Twayne Publishers, 1961; 2nd ed. rev., Boston: Twayne Publishers, 1975. Both are part of the publisher's United States Authors Series. The texts, however, are different, and the present book does not entirely supersede either.

Gray, James. *John Steinbeck.* Minneapolis: University of Minnesota Pamphlets on American Writers, no. 94, 1971. A brief tribute to Steinbeck as an "ecologist."

Hayashi, Tetsumaro, ed. *John Steinbeck: A Guide to the Doctoral Dissertations.* Muncie, Ind.: Steinbeck Monograph Series, no. 1, 1971. Includes abstracts of 16 doctoral dissertations approved between 1946 and 1969.

————, ed. *John Steinbeck: The Years of Greatness, 1936–1939.* Tuscaloosa: University of Alabama Press, 1993. The papers presented by the 10 American participants in the Third International John Steinbeck Congress, Honolulu, 27–30 May 1990.

————, ed. *Steinbeck and the Arthurian Theme.* Steinbeck Monograph Series, No. 5. Muncie, Ind.: The John Steinbeck Society of America, 1975. Essays by Warren French, Arthur F. Kinney, and Roy S. Simmonds on Steinbeck's use of Sir Thomas Malory's *Morte d'Arthur.*

————, ed. *Steinbeck Criticism: A Review of Book-Length Studies.* Steinbeck Monograph Series, No. 4. Muncie, Ind.: The John Steinbeck Society of America, 1974. Gathers new and revised reviews of 17 books listed elsewhere in this bibliography that had been published about Steinbeck by 1973.

————, and Kenneth D. Swan, eds. *Steinbeck's Prophetic Vision of America.* Upland, Ind.: Taylor University, 1976. The American "Bicentennial Essays on John Steinbeck," delivered at Taylor University, 1 May 1976. Includes papers by the editors and Warren French's "Steinbeck and Modernism."

Jain, Sunita. *Steinbeck's Concept of Man*. New Delhi: New Statesman, 1979. An ambitious tribute attempting to demonstrate that Steinbeck's concept of man's "struggling to attain dignity by imposing order on his dual existence as an individual and a group animal" remains consistent throughout his career.

Jones, Lawrence William. *John Steinbeck as Fabulist*. Edited by Marston LaFrance. Steinbeck Monograph Series, No. 3. Muncie, Ind.: The John Steinbeck Society of America, 1973. One of the indispensable books about Steinbeck by a young scholar who was tragically killed before its publication; Jones uses Sheldon Sack's techniques for classifying fiction to demonstrate Steinbeck's increasing penchant for parable writing after World War II.

Levant, Howard. *The Novels of John Steinbeck*. Columbia: University of Missouri Press, 1974. Studies Steinbeck's fiction in terms of his use of "dramatic" and "panoramic" techniques," especially as these relate to increasing problems in finding forms to embody his personal philosophy.

Lewis, Cliff, and Carroll Britch, eds. *Rediscovering Steinbeck: Revisionist Views of His Art, Politics, and Intellect*. Lewiston, N.Y.: Edwin Mellen Press, 1989. A collection of original essays, often about Steinbeck's more obscure works, tracing the evolution of his art and social perspectives.

Lisca, Peter. *John Steinbeck: Nature and Myth*. New York: Crowell, 1978. An enchanting introduction for young readers by the scholar who rediscovered an undervalued Steinbeck. Finds his "unique genius" in his ability to depict man living in both the natural and the mythical worlds, "without distorting either."

————. *The Wide World of John Steinbeck*. New Brunswick, N.J.: Rutgers University Press, 1958. The first detailed critical appraisal of Steinbeck for nearly 20 years, at a time when his reputation had seriously declined; provides the first close reading in the then dominant New Critical fashion that Lisca thought the fiction deserved and that did much to claim for Steinbeck a place among the most important American novelists.

McCarthy, Paul. *John Steinbeck*. New York: Ungar, 1980. A most useful book for those seeking a concise overview of Steinbeck's writings and major criticisms of them in an intelligent and sympathetic synthesis.

Marks, Lester Jay. *Thematic Design in the Novels of John Steinbeck*. The Hague: Mouton, 1969. The most enthusiastic Steinbeck critic finds *East of Eden* the climax of the novelist's consistent thematic development in a search for values.

Moore, Harry Thornton. *The Novels of John Steinbeck: A First Critical Study*. Chicago: Normandie House, 1939; reissued with an afternote, Port Washington, N.Y.: Kennikat Press, 1968. This inaugural study of Steinbeck by a distinguished D. H. Lawrence scholar, who subsequently lost interest in Steinbeck, introduced the author of *The Grapes of Wrath* to an audience who knew little of him.

Nakayama, Kiyoshi, Scott Pugh, and Shigeharu Yano, eds. *John Steinbeck: Asian Perspectives*. Osaka, Japan: Osaka Kyoiku Tosho, 1992. Collects papers presented by Asian scholars on Steinbeck and Oriental thought and other topics reflecting Japanese, Korean, Thai, and Indian interest in the author at the Third International Steinbeck Congress, Honolulu, 1990. Published in English.

Owens, Louis. *John Steinbeck's Re-vision of America*. Athens: University of Georgia Press, 1939. This first detailed critique to appear after Benson's biography concentrates on Steinbeck's California novels in which he seeks to illuminate "the way out of the American wasteland."

Pratt, John Clark. *John Steinbeck: A Critical Essay*. Grand Rapids, Mich.: Eerdmans, 1970. Part of a series on "Contemporary Writers in Christian Perspectives," this pamphlet discusses Steinbeck's use of religious elements in "syncretic allegories."

Satyanarayana, M. R. *John Steinbeck: A Study in the Theme of Compassion*. Hyderabad: Osmania University Press, 1977. An Indian scholar concludes that, though Steinbeck is unhappy about man's inhumanity to man, "he believes that the evil of violence and hatred can be cured by love and understanding."

Sharma, R, K., ed. *Indian Response to Steinbeck: Essays Presented to Warren French*. Jaipur: Rachana Prakashan, 1984. A collection of seven general estimates of Steinbeck's work and 18 essays on individual novels that illustrates the writer's international influence.

Shimomura, Noboru. *A Study of John Steinbeck: Mysticism in His Novels*. Tokyo: Hokuseido Press, 1982. A study of Steinbeck's use of Christian and Oriental mystical doctrines in all of his fiction, moving from pagan to conventional Christian mysticism at the end of his career.

Simmonds, Roy S. *Steinbeck's Literary Achievement* Steinbeck Monograph Series, No. 6. Muncie, Ind.: The John Steinbeck Society of America, 1976. Working in the now uncommon traditional genre of an "appreciation," an English scholar investigates Steinbeck's major themes, humor, style, sources, and influences in the best introduction that has been written to the serious reading and understanding of the fiction.

Tedlock, Ernest W. Jr., and C. V. Wicker, eds. *Steinbeck and His Critics: A Record of Twenty-five Years*. Albuquerque: University of New Mexico Press, 1958. This first compilation of writings about Steinbeck reprints essays of continuing value from the 1930s and 1940s, along with Peter Lisca's survey of scholarship preceding the publication of his first book.

Timmerman, John. *John Steinbeck's Fiction: The Aesthetics of the Road Taken*. Norman: University of Oklahoma Press, 1986. In an effort to reconcile Steinbeck to conservative readers, Timmerman returns to the oversimplified view that "the philosophy of Naturalism constitutes Steinbeck's essential view of humanity" and that he "operates solidly within the framework of his literary precursors."

Watt, F. W. *John Steinbeck.* Edinburgh: Oliver & Boyd; New York: Grove Press, 1962. A thin but sophisticated introduction of Steinbeck to European readers, stressing his regionalism and the "nonteleological" thinking shaping his fiction.

Yano, Shigeharu. *The Current of Steinbeck's World 1–5.* Tokyo: Seibido, 1978–86. A series of fascicles bringing together individual essays on Steinbeck's writings in no particular order. Yano has provided no general essay synthesizing his views, but the emphasis throughout these meditations that provide an excellent insight into an Oriental reading of Steinbeck is on man's spiritual awakening—the theme pursued most assiduously by Asian authors.

Books on Individual Books

The Grapes of Wrath

Bloom, Harold, ed. *John Steinbeck's "The Grapes of Wrath."* Modern Critical Interpretations. New York: Chelsea House, 1988. Part of a series on great books, introduced by the Yale critic and reprinting eight essays on the novel in chronological order from 1942 to 1985.

Davis, Robert Con. *Twentieth Century Interpretations of "The Grapes of Wrath."* Englewood Cliffs, N.J.: Prentice Hall, 1982. Reprints 11 chapters from books and journal articles with a previously unpublished essay by Joan Hedrick.

Ditsky, John, ed. *Critical Essays on Steinbeck's "The Grapes of Wrath."* Boston: G. K. Hall, 1989. A meticulously planned and presented collection of 10 1939 reviews of the novel, followed by five major reprinted essays and four essays especially commissioned for the volume.

Donohue, Agnes McNeil, ed. *A Casebook on "The Grapes of Wrath."* New York: Crowell, 1968. A hefty compendium of practically all useful criticism of the novel published before the author's death in a then popular format for providing students with material for research papers.

French, Warren, ed. *A Companion to "The Grapes of Wrath."* New York: Viking Press, 1963. Reprints *Their Blood Is Strong,* Steinbeck's 1936 newspaper reports on migrant laborers, along with material on the background, reception, and reputation of the novel.

Hayashi, Tetsumaro, ed. *"The Grapes of Wrath: Essays in Criticism.* Steinbeck Essay Series No. 3 Muncie, Ind.: The Steinbeck Research Institute, 1990. Eight essays from the *Steinbeck Quarterly,* reprinted in conjunction with the fiftieth anniversary of the publication of the novel.

Owens, Louis. *"The Grapes of Wrath": Trouble in the Promised Land.* Boston: Twayne Publishers, 1989. Published during the fiftieth anniversary of the publication of the novel, this is part of a "Masterworks" series, designed to incorporate information about the background and history of the novel with a contemporary reading of it for educational libraries.

Shillinglaw, Susan, ed. *"The Grapes of Wrath:* A Special Issue." *San Jose Studies* 17, no. 1 (Winter 1990). Entirely devoted to papers presented at an interdisciplinary forum at San Jose State University, California, celebrating the fiftieth anniversary of the publication of the novel, 16–18 March 1989.

Wyatt, David, ed. *New Essays on "The Grapes of Wrath."* Cambridge, Mass.: Cambridge University Press, 1990. Part of a series on American novels that seeks to promote new techniques and directions in literary criticism, this volume presents four commissioned essays, by critics who had not previously published on Steinbeck, about the novel's portrayal of women, its roots in journalism, and its film adaptation, stressing issues of race, class, and gender.

The Long Valley (and uncollected short stories)

Hayashi, Tetsumaro, ed. *Steinbeck's Short Stories in "The Long Valley": Essays in Criticism.* Muncie, Ind.: The Steinbeck Research Institute, 1991. A new collection of specially commissioned essays on all the stories in the book, except *The Red Pony* group, with an introduction by Warren French and "Steinbeck as Short Story Writer" by Robert S. Hughes, Jr.

————, ed. *A Study Guide to Steinbeck's "The Long Valley."* Ann Arbor, Mich.: Pierian Press, 1976. A collection of articles by a number of Steinbeck critics on individual stories from 1972–73 issues of *Steinbeck Quarterly,* reprinted with an essay on "Steinbeck as a Short Story Writer" by Brian Barbour.

Hughes, Robert S. *Beyond "The Red Pony": A Reader's Companion to Steinbeck's Complete Short Stories.* Metuchen, N.J.: Scarecrow Press, 1986.

————. *John Steinbeck: A Study of the Short Fiction.* Boston: Twayne Publishers, 1989. In the earlier book Hughes discusses the stories in *The Long Valley,* as well as uncollected pieces from early years, chapters from *The Grapes of Wrath,* and reports from *Once There Was a War* that can be read as short stories. In the later book, part of a series on short fiction, he also discusses *The Pastures of Heaven* as a story-cycle and includes statements on writing by Steinbeck and four articles by other critics.

Timmerman, John H. *The Dramatic Landscape of Steinbeck's Short Stories.* Norman: University of Oklahoma Press, 1990. A valuable study for Steinbeck specialists on the development of his artistry that makes extensive use of the notebooks in which he wrote the first drafts of his stories; it is not as comprehensive as Hughes's books, however.

The Moon Is Down

Coers, Donald V., *John Steinbeck as Propagandist: "The Moon Is Down" Goes to War.* Tuscaloosa: University of Alabama Press, 1991. The first thoroughly documented account of the differing receptions of this controversial novel in the United States and in the occupied countries of Europe, particularly

Norway, Denmark, France, and the Netherlands, drawing on many interviews with the last survivors of the period.

Hayashi, Tetsumaro. *Steinbeck's World War II Fiction, "The Moon Is Down": Three Explications.* Steinbeck Essay Series, No. 1. Muncie, Ind.: The Steinbeck Research Institute, 1986. A Shakespearean specialist defends the novelette/play's portrayal of people's "indomitable will to preserve their traditional democratic values against totalitarianism, oppression and slavery," especially through comparisons with *Macbeth.*

The Pastures of Heaven

Fontenrose, Joseph. *Steinbeck's Unhappy Valley.* Berkeley, Calif., 1981. An erudite interpretation of the story cycle by the distinguished California classicist, arguing that the "curse" the Munroes bring on the beautiful valley results from their representing " 'progress' and conformity, the outside world coming in," threatening those who wish to evade it.

The Red Pony

Hayashi, Tetsumaro, and Thomas J. Moore, eds. *Steinbeck's "The Red Pony": Essays in Criticism.* Steinbeck Monograph Series, no. 13. Muncie, Ind.: The Steinbeck Research Institute, 1988. Individual essays on the four stories in the cycle, contributed by Thomas M. Tammaro, Robert S. Hughes, Jr., Roy S. Simmonds, and Mimi R. Gladstein, with an introduction by Warren French.

Film Studies

Burrows, Michael. *John Steinbeck and His Films.* St. Austell, Cornwall: Primestyle, 1970. Reprints comments and criticisms from many sources, along with stills from the films.

French, Warren. *A Filmguide to "The Grapes of Wrath."* Bloomington: Indiana University Press, 1973. Provides information and comments for the study of the film as both an adaptation of the novel and an autonomous work of art.

Millichap, Joseph R. *Steinbeck and Film.* New York: Ungar, 1983. Provides thorough histories of the productions and analyses of all the films, including television adaptations, derived from Steinbeck's writings in chronological order to *Cannery Row* (1982), emphasizing the superiority of the early *Of Mice and Men* and *The Grapes of Wrath.*

Background Readings

French, Warren. *The Social Novel at the End of an Era.* Carbondale: Southern Illinois University Press, 1966. In a study of outstanding social novels published in 1939, French provides a long section on Steinbeck's relationship to the "mystical agragriansim" of the "back to the land" movement flourishing during the depression.

Gregory, James N. *American Exodus: The Dust Bowl and Okie Culture in California.* New York: Oxford University Press, 1989. Provides a detailed account of the Dust Bowl of the 1930s and the migration to California depicted in *The Grapes of Wrath.*

Haslam, Gerald. *Coming of Age in California: Personal Essays.* Walnut Creek, Calif.: Devil Mountain Books, 1990.

———. *Voices of a Place: Social and Literary Essays from the Other California.* Walnut Creek, Calif.: Devil Mountain Books, 1987. Two autobiographical volumes by one of the most gifted California fictionists of the generation succeeding Steinbeck, sharing his experiences growing up in the San Joaquin Valley in central California, where the California-born progeny of Steinbeck's Okies have settled.

McWilliams, Carey. *Factories in the Fields.* Boston: Little, Brown, 1939. Published in the same year as *The Grapes of Wrath,* this is the complementary factual study by the then California Commission of Immigration and Housing of the plight of the migrant workers.

Journals

American Literary Scholarship has been published annually since 1963 by Duke University Press (Durham, N.C.). A changing roster of general editors and specialist scholars review the year's work in American literature in this country and abroad; includes summaries and comments on Steinbeck studies.

Steinbeck Newsletter, edited by Susan Shillinglaw, director of the Steinbeck Research Institute at San Jose State University, California, has appeared semi-annually since 1987, carrying short articles, reviews, and news reports of interest to Steinbeck's audience.

Steinbeck Quarterly, originally *Steinbeck Newsletter,* edited by Tetsumaro Hayashi, was for 25 years (1968–93), the official organ of The International John Steinbeck Society, founded by Hayashi to encourage Steinbeck scholarship and provide material of interest to Steinbeck readers and scholars. Following Hayashi's retirement, publication has been temporarily suspended.

Index

The Author

Warren French is an honorary professor of American studies at the University of Wales, Swansea. He received his B.A. from the University of Pennsylvania and his M.A. and Ph.D. in American literature and history from the University of Texas–Austin. He taught at the Universities of Mississippi, Kentucky, Florida, and Missouri–Kansas City, and also at Stetson University and Kansas State University before becoming chair of the Department of English and director of American studies at Indiana University, Indianapolis, from which he retired in 1986. He is the author of two earlier books on John Steinbeck, *Frank Norris, J. D. Salinger* and *J. D. Salinger Revisited, Jack Kerouac* and *The San Francisco Poetry Renaissance, 1955–1960* in Twayne's United States Authors Series. He has also edited the books on contemporary American literature in this series between 1975 and 1990 and Twayne's Filmmakers Series. He is also the author of *The Social Novel at the End of an Era* and the editor of four volumes on American fiction, poetry, and drama from the 1920s to the 1950s and also *A Companion to "The Grapes of Wrath"* and *The South in Film.*

The Editor

Frank Day is a professor of English at Clemson University. He is the author of *Sir William Empson: An Annotated Bibliography* and *Arthur Koestler: A Guide to Research*. He was a Fulbright lecturer in American literature in Romania (1980–81) and in Bangladesh (1986–87).